Mental Arithmetic 6

Name of student

....

Diagnostic Chart for

Indicate where the studen

Test	Part	1	2	3	4	5	6	7					
Test 1	Part A												
	Part B												
	Part C												
Test 2	Part A												
	Part B												
	Part C												
Test 3	Part A												
	Part B												
	Part C												
Test 4	Part A												
	Part B												
	Part C												
Test 5	Part A												
	Part B												
	Part C												
Test 6	Part A												
	Part B												
	Part C												
Test 7	Part A												
	Part B												
	Part C												
Test 8	Part A												
	Part B												
	Part C												
Test 9	Part A												
	Part B												
	Part C												
Test 10	Part A												
	Part B												
	Part C												
Test 11	Part A												
	Part B												
	Part C												
Test 12	Part A												
	Part B												
	Part C												

Section 1 Test 1

A

ANSWER

1	154 + 67 =	221
2	(2 × 45) + (1 × 45) =	135
3	Write in figures the number one thousand one hundred and one.	1101
4	33% is larger than $\frac{1}{3}$ TRUE or FALSE?	FALSE
5	Write as a decimal $5 + \frac{5}{100}$.	5.05
6	1.59 + 0.73 =	2.32
7	1.5 × (1.5 + 2.5) =	6
8	Approximate 7846 to the nearest thousand.	8000
9	(a) Calculate exactly, then (b) approximate to 1 decimal place 8.64 ÷ 4	(a) 2.16 (b) 2.2
10	If $a = 2$, $b = 5$, find the value of $3a + b$.	11
11	$4m = 10$, so $m =$	2.5
12	$6^2 =$	36

B

ANSWER

1	86p + 35p + 71p =	£ 1·92
2	Find 8% of £5.	40p
3	Change 317 mm to cm.	31.7 cm
4	510 mm + 815 mm	= 1 m 325 mm = 1.325 m
5	90 days =	12 weeks 6 days
6	An aeroplane flies 3900 km in 6 hours. What is its mean (average) speed?	650 km/h
7	Find the perimeter of a rectangular field measuring 35 m by 22 m.	114 m
8	What size is the interior angle in each corner of an equilateral triangle?	60°
9	Which letters of the word WAIST have at least one axis of symmetry?	W, A, I, T
10	Approximate £13·63 to the nearest £1.	£ 14

C

ANSWER

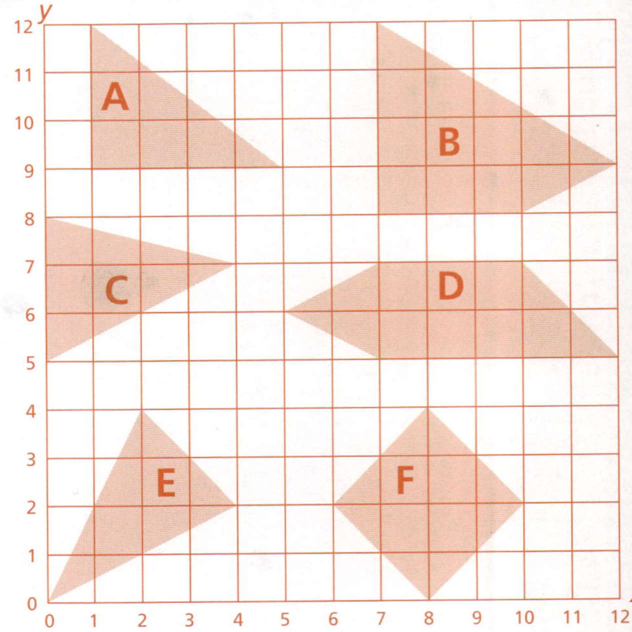

1	Write down the coordinates of each corner of triangle *A*.	(1 , 9)
2		(1 , 12)
3		(5 , 9)
4	Write down the coordinates of the two corners of quadrilateral *B* that have the same *x*-value as each other.	(7 , 8)
5		(7 , 12)
6	Write down the coordinates of the corner of the triangle *C* that has the largest *y*-value.	(0 , 8)
7	Write down the coordinates of the corner of the pentagon *D* that has the smallest *x*-value.	(5 , 6)
8	Write down the coordinates of the corner of triangle *E* whose *x*-value is twice the corresponding *y*-value.	(4 , 2)
9	Write down the coordinates of the mid-point of the shortest side of triangle *E*.	(3 , 3)
10	Write down the coordinates of the point where the diagonals of square *F* intersect each other.	(8 , 2)
11	Estimate the coordinates of the mid-point of the longest side of triangle *A*.	(3 , 10.5)
12	Estimate the coordinates of the mid-point of the longest side of quadrilateral *B*.	(9.5 , 10.5)

Section 1 Test 2

A

ANSWER

1 154 − 67 = 87

2 (4 × 33) − 33 = 99

3 Write in figures the number five hundred and five thousand five hundred. 505 500

4 $\frac{3}{8}$ < 50% TRUE or FALSE? TRUE

5 Write as a decimal $\frac{5}{100} + \frac{8}{1000}$. 0.058

6 2.07 − 0.09 = 1.98

7 6.4 ÷ (2.5 − 0.9) = 4

8 Approximate 8079 to the nearest hundred. 8100

9 (a) Calculate exactly, then (b) approximate to 1 decimal place

15.165 ÷ 3 (a) 5.055 (b) 5.1

10 If $x = 4$ and $y = 3$, find the value of xy. 12

11 $5p + 2.5 = 10$, so $p =$ 1.5

12 $15^2 =$ 225

B

ANSWER

1 £1·27 + 55p = £ 1·82

2 What is 6.5% of £40? £ 2·60

3 Change 455 g to kg. 0.455 kg

4 850 cm + 2.53 m = 1103 cm
= 11.03 m

5 120 weeks = 2 years 16 weeks

6 A wooden block slides 90 cm in half a minute. Find its mean (average) speed in cm/s. 3 cm/s

7 Find the area of a footpath 0.8 km long and 1.2 m wide. 960 m^2

8 What size is the interior angle of each corner of a square? 90°

9 Which letters of the word WAIST have more than one axis of symmetry? I

10 Approximate 1858 mm to the nearest metre. 2 m

C

ANSWER

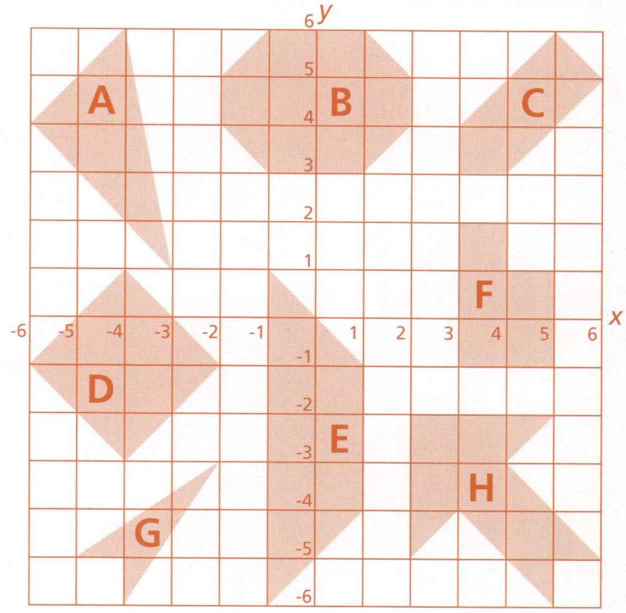

1 Write the coordinates of each corner of the trapezium E. (−1 , 1) (1 , −1) (1 , −4) (−1 , −6)

2 Which shape has corner coordinates whose x-values are all positive and whose y-values are all positive? C

3 Which shape has corner coordinates whose x-values are all positive and whose y-values are all negative? H

4 Which shape has corner coordinates whose x-values are all negative and whose y-values are all positive? A

5 Which shape has corner coordinates whose x-values are all negative and whose y-values are all negative? G

6 Write the coordinates of the corner of square D that have the most negative y-value. (−4 , −3)

7 Write down the coordinates of the corner of square D that has the most negative x-value. (−6 , −1)

8 Which shape has the same area as H? D

9 Which shape has half the area of B? F

10 Which shape has one side that passes through the origin? E

11 The coordinates of one corner of shape B have a y-value that is twice the corresponding x-value. Write down the coordinates of this corner. (2 , 4)

12 The x-value and the y-value of the coordinates of two corners of shape H add up to zero. Write down the coordinates of these two corners. (2 , −2) (5 , −5)

Section 1 Test 3

A

ANSWER

1 $154 \times 7 =$ 1078

2 $(56 + 35) \div 7 =$ 13

3 Write in figures three-quarters of a million. 750 000

4 $17\% > 0.17$ TRUE or FALSE? FALSE

5 Write as a decimal $\frac{15}{100} + \frac{15}{1000}$. 0.165

6 $6.5 \times 20 =$ 130

7 $1.5 + (0.75 \times 4) =$ 4.5

8 Approximate 6.26 to the nearest tenth. 6.3

9 (a) Calculate exactly, then
(b) approximate to 1 decimal place

$36.108 \div 6$ (a) 6.018 (b) 6.0

10 If $p = 3$ and $q = 8$, find the value of $3p + 2 - q$. 3

11 $\frac{a}{5} = 15$, so $a =$ 75

12 $\sqrt{64} =$ 8

B

ANSWER

1 91p – 55p + 14p = £ 0·50

2 Find 3.5% of £7000. £ 245

3 Change 650 mℓ to litres. 0.650 ℓ

4 2148 mm + 967 mm = 3 m 115 mm
= 3.115 m

5 65 decades = 650 years

6 Abdul runs 100 m in 12.5 s. What is his mean (average) speed in m/s? 8 m/s

7 What size is the circumference of a circle of 80 m diameter? $\pi = 3.14$ 251.2 m

8 At what angle do the diagonals of a square cross each other? 90°

9 Which letters of the word MONEY have one, and only one, axis of symmetry? M, E, Y

10 Approximate 88 inches to the nearest foot. 7 ft

C

ANSWER

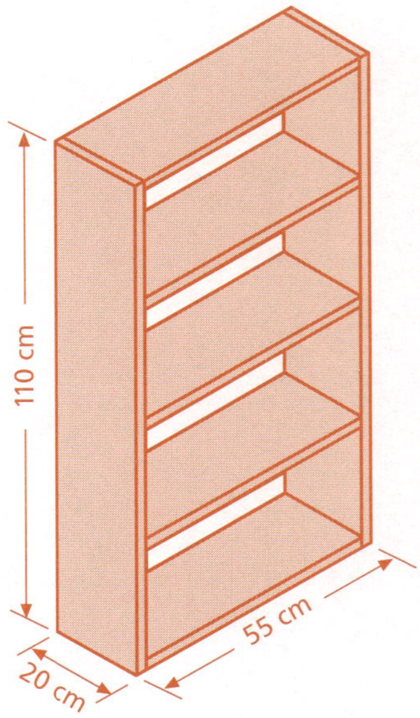

Nathan wants to make a bookcase for his bedroom. It is to be 110 cm high and will contain four rows of books. Each shelf will be 55 cm long. The planks of wood he intends to use to make the bookcase are 20 cm wide and 2 cm thick. Each plank when bought is 250 cm long and costs £3·00 per metre length.

1 What will it cost to buy each plank of wood? £ 7·50

2 How many planks will be needed for the two sides? 1

3 How many planks will be needed for the top, bottom and the shelves? 2

4 What is the total number of planks needed to make the bookcase? 3

5 How much will it cost to buy all the wood needed to make the bookcase? £ 22·50

6 How wide will the finished bookcase be, allowing for the thickness of the sides? 59 cm

7 What will be the total length of shelves on which books can be placed? 220 cm

8 If the shelves are evenly spaced what is the size of the tallest book that will fit on a shelf? 25 cm

9 Nathan has a lot of books that are 25 mm thick. How many of these books will fit on each shelf? 22

10 How many of these books will fit into the whole bookcase? 88

11 What is the total length of wood used to make the bookcase? 495 cm

12 Approximately what length of wood will Nathan have left over in total? 255 cm

Section 1 Test 4

A

ANSWER

1 $154 \div 7 =$ 22

2 $(11 \times 9) + (0 \times 9) =$ 99

3 Write in words the number 60060. sixty thousand and sixty

4 Write the fraction $\frac{3}{20}$ as a percentage. 15%

5 Express 20% of 0.25 as a decimal. 0.05

6 $4.5 \div 6 =$ 0.75

7 $10 - (6.3 \div 10) =$ 9.37

8 Approximate 0.044 to the nearest hundredth. 0.04

9 (a) Calculate exactly, then (b) approximate to 1 decimal place.
2.1×3.2 (a) 6.72 (b) 6.7

10 If $s = 6$ and $t = 5$, find the value of $3t - 2s$. 3

11 $\frac{12}{x} = 2.4$, so $x =$ 5

12 $\sqrt{144} =$ 12

B

ANSWER

1 £13·26 – 115p = £ 12·11

2 What is 17.5% of £50? £ 8·75

3 Change 2.5 m to cm. 250 cm

4 2650 m + 8145 m = 10 km 795 m
= 10.795 km

5 $3\frac{1}{2}$ centuries = 350 years

6 Katy cycles $4\frac{1}{2}$ miles in 20 minutes. Find her mean (average) speed in mph. $13\frac{1}{2}$ mph

7 Find the circumference of a coin whose diameter is 2.5 cm
$\pi = 3.14$ 7.85 cm

8 The smallest angle of a right-angled triangle is 30°. What sizes are the other angles? 90°, 60°

9 Which letters of the word VAPOUR have a vertical axis of symmetry? V, A, O, U

10 Approximate 606 g to the nearest kg. 1 kg

C

ANSWER

The table below is part of a computer. spreadsheet. The computer can perform calculations on the data held in each cell by applying a mathematical formula. For example, the value in cell D2 is found by using the formula B2*C2 where * means multiply (i.e. £6·50 = £0·65 × 10).

The formula used to calculate the total cost of £47·02 is SUM(D2:D9). That is, £47·02 is found by adding together all the values in cells D2 to D9.

	A	B	C	D
1	Goods ordered	Price each	Quantity	Cost
2	13 amp plug	£0·65	10	£6·50
3	Single socket	£1·99	6	£11·94
4	Double socket	£2·99	4	£11·96
5	Single switch	£0·99	5	£4·95
6	Double switch	£1·49	2	£2·98
7	Two-way switch	£2·49	1	£2·49
8	60 watt bulb	£0·45	4	£1·80
9	100 watt bulb	£0·55	8	£4·40
10	Total			£47·02

1 Write down the contents of cell A5. Single switch

2 Write down the contents of cell B9. £ 0·55

3 Write down the contents of cell D4. £ 11·96

4 Which cell contains the words "60 watt bulb"? A8

5 Which cell contains the value 8? C9

6 Which cell contains the value £2·98? D6

7 What is the result of multiplying the contents of cell B8 by the contents of cell C8? £ 1·80

8 Which cell of the table above contains the answer to Question 7? D8

9 What is the result of applying the formula B5*C5? £ 4·95

10 What is the result of applying the formula SUM(C2:C9) 40

11 Into which empty cell would you write the answer to Question 10? C10

12 Write down in words what the result of the formula in Question 10 tells you.
total quantity of goods ordered is 40

Section 1 Test 5

A

		ANSWER
1	1001 × 13 =	13 013
2	154 ÷ 25 =	6 rem 4
3	Add together two thousand and eight and eight thousand and two. Answer in figures.	10 010
4	Express 2% as a decimal.	0.02
5	Write $\frac{3}{5}$ of 7.5 as a decimal.	4.5
6	21.3 – 7.8 + 8.7 =	22.2
7	9.9 – (9.9 ÷ 9.9) =	8.9
8	Approximate 14.139 to two decimal places.	14.14
9	(a) Calculate exactly, then (b) approximate to 1 decimal place. 0.05 x 3.22	(a) 0.161 (b) 0.2
10	If $x = 40$, $y = 50$, find the value of $3(y - x)$.	30
11	$3a + 5 = 29$, so $a =$	8
12	$2^3 =$	8

B

		ANSWER
1	81p – £1·06 + 52p =	27p
2	Increase £25 by 40%.	£ 35
3	Change 1.1 kg to g.	1100 g
4	855 g + 2.2 kg	= 3 kg 55 g = 3.055 kg
5	4 h 20 min =	260 min
6	Nathan runs 60 m in 10 seconds. Find his mean (average) speed in km/h.	21.6 km/h
7	Find the area in ha of a rectangular field 250 m long and 80 m wide.	2 ha
8	The largest angle of an isosceles triangle is 100°. How big is each of the other angles?	40°
9	Which letters of the word GROCER have a horizontal axis of symmetry?	O , C , E
10	Approximate 50 oz to the nearest lb.	3 lb

C

ANSWER

The table compares monthly rainfall figures for Glasgow and London.

	Rainfall in mm	
Month	**Glasgow**	**London**
January	170	45
February	141	39
March	127	44
April	88	36
May	86	43
June	79	49
July	99	63
August	135	58
September	119	48
October	133	65
November	161	54
December	186	56
Annual total	1524	600

		ANSWER
1	What is the total annual rainfall for Glasgow?	1524 mm
2	What is the mean (average) monthly rainfall for Glasgow?	127 mm
3	In which month was the rainfall in Glasgow closest to the mean?	March
4	What fraction of Glasgow's annual rainfall fell in March?	$\frac{1}{12}$
5	What is the RANGE of rainfall in Glasgow? (i.e. the difference between the wettest month and the driest month)	107 mm
6	By how much does the rainfall in Glasgow's driest month exceed that of London's wettest month?	14 mm
7	What is the total annual rainfall for London?	600 mm
8	What is the mean (average) monthly rainfall for London?	50 mm
9	In which month was the rainfall in London closest to the mean?	June
10	What percentage of London's annual rainfall fell in the driest month?	6%
11	What is the RANGE of rainfall in London?	29 mm
12	What is the ratio of Glasgow's annual rainfall to that of London? (express your answer as a percentage)	254%

Section 1 Test 6

A

		ANSWER
1	$1001 \div 13 =$	77
2	$(50 \times 6) + (4 \times 50) =$	500
3	$(5 \times 10^3) + (2 \times 10^2) + (0 \times 10) + (5 \times 1) =$	5205
4	Write 0.45 as a fraction in its lowest terms.	$\frac{9}{20}$
5	What number is 30% more than 1000?	1300
6	$14.4 \div 1.2 =$	12
7	$8.8 - (8.8 \div 8) =$	7.7
8	Approximate 0.097 to two decimal places.	0.10
9	Work out correct to two decimal places 5.271 + 1.527	6.80
10	If $u = 9$, $a = 2.5$, $t = 2$, find the value of $u + at$.	14
11	$2t - 7 = 5$, $t =$	6
12	$5^3 =$	125

B

		ANSWER
1	21p × 5 =	£ 1·05
2	Reduce £120 by 10%.	£ 108
3	Change $\frac{1}{2}$ litre to mℓ.	500 mℓ
4	6000 kg + 3.5 t =	9 t 500 kg
	=	9.5 t
5	36 hours =	$1\frac{1}{2}$ days
6	Oil flowing in a pipe takes 15 s to travel 21 cm. Find its speed in mm/s.	14 mm/s
7	Find the area in m^2 of a stone slab 90 cm by 60 cm.	0.54 m^2
8	At what angle do the diagonals of a rhombus cross each other?	90°
9	Which letters of the word MUSIC remain the same after a rotation about the centre by 180°?	S , I
10	Approximate 22 000 cm^2 to the nearest m^2.	2 m^2

C

ANSWER

The diagram shows a plan of a two-bedroomed bungalow. The grid lines are spaced 1 cm apart.

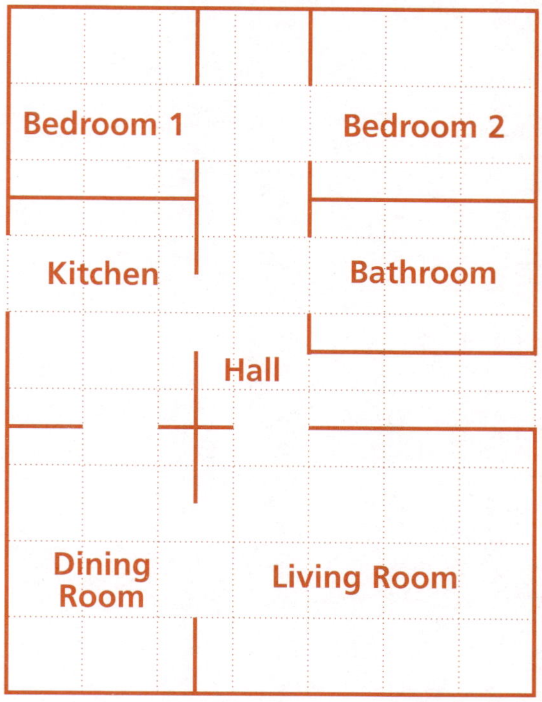

Scale 1:100

		ANSWER
1	What length is represented by 1 cm on the plan?	1 m
2	What size is bedroom 1?	2.5 m by 2.5 m
3	What is the area of bedroom 1?	6.25 m^2
4	What size is bedroom 2?	3 m by 2.5 m
5	What is the area of bedroom 2?	7.5 m^2
6	What is the cost of carpeting both bedrooms at £10 per square metre?	£ 137·50
7	What is the cost of carpeting the living room at £20 per square metre?	£ 315
8	How many tiles 250 mm square will be needed to cover the kitchen floor?	120
9	How much will they cost if tiles are 80p each?	£ 96
10	The bath takes up 22% of the floor area of the bathroom. What is the area of the bath?	1.32 m^2
11	Which has the bigger area, the hall or the dining room, and by how much?	dining room by 0.5 m^2
12	What is the perimeter of the bungalow?	32 m

Section 1 Test 7

A

		ANSWER
1	67 + 54 + 33 =	154
2	(540 ÷ 9) ÷ 9 =	6 rem 6
3	$(3 \times 10^4) + (2 \times 10^3) =$	32 000
4	Express 250% as a mixed number.	$2\frac{1}{2}$
5	Add 20% of 35 to 18% of 200.	43
6	1.27 – 5.03 + 4.85 =	1.09
7	(2.5 – 1.0) × (2.5 + 1.0) =	5.25
8	Approximate 7.0826 to three decimal places.	7.083
9	Work out correct to two decimal places 0.72 × 2.7	1.94
10	If $l = 12$, $b = 6$, $h = 4$ find the value of lbh.	288
11	$\frac{w}{4} + \frac{1}{2} = 2$, so $w =$	6
12	List the factors of 24.	1, 2, 3, 4, 6, 8, 12, 24

B

		ANSWER
1	£3·06 × 6 =	£ 18·36
2	How much interest at 5% is given on £600?	£ 30
3	Change 3170 mm to m.	3.17 m
4	660 mℓ × 5	= 3 ℓ 300 mℓ = 3.3 ℓ
5	Write in 24-hour-clock notation 25 minutes to 1 pm.	12.35
6	How long will it take to walk 112 miles at a rate of 8 miles/day?	14 days
7	A tank 1.2 m tall has a base of area 0.6 m^2. Find its volume.	0.72 m^3
8	What size is the interior angle of each corner of a regular pentagon?	108°
9	If the word DOZEN is turned upside down, which letters look the same?	O, Z, N
10	Approximate 940 000 cm^3 to the nearest cubic metre.	1 m^3

C

Abdul keeps a record of the number of times different kinds of birds visit his garden. Over a period of two days Abdul observed a total of 60 birds. He drew a graph to show the results.

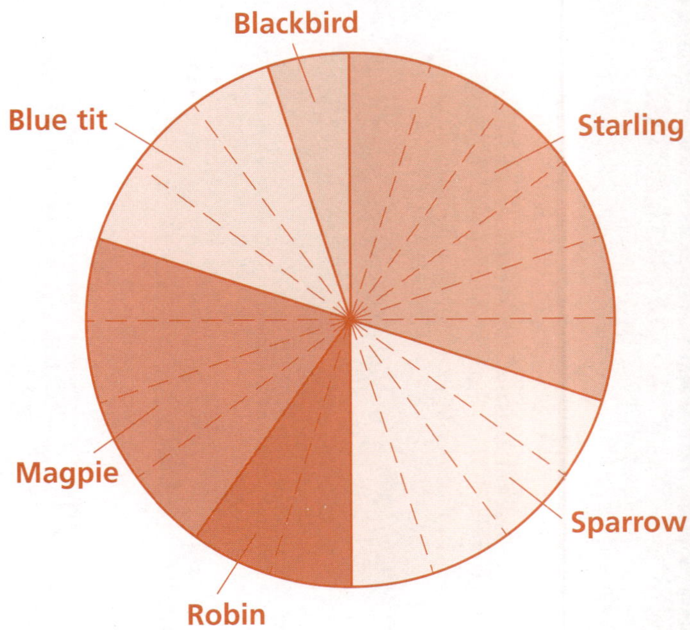

		ANSWER
1	Which type of bird came to Abdul's garden most often?	starling
2	Which type of bird was the least frequent visitor?	blackbird
3	Which two birds visited in equal numbers?	magpie, sparrow
4	What percentage of the total visits were made by robins?	10%
5	What percentage of the total visits were made by starlings?	30%
6	Five percent of the total visits were made by which bird?	blackbird
7	Which bird made 15% of the visits in the two-day period?	blue tit
8	Which bird made 50% of the number of visits made by sparrows?	robin
9	What was the number of magpies that came during the two days?	12
10	How many more sparrows than blue tits came to Abdul's garden?	3
11	How many times could Abdul expect to see a robin if he continued his observations for a full week?	21
12	Estimate the total number of birds that Abdul might expect to see in his garden in a week?	210

Section 1 Test 8

A

ANSWER

		ANSWER
1	67 + 54 − 21 =	100
2	540 ÷ (9 ÷ 9) =	540
3	2.5×10^2 =	250
4	Write 31.5% as a decimal.	0.315
5	Express 24% of $\frac{1}{2}$ as a decimal.	0.12
6	0.2 × 0.2 =	0.04
7	(3.6 ÷ 1.2) × (3.6 + 1.2) =	14.4
8	Approximate 623 to two significant figures.	620
9	Work out correct to two significant figures 0.72 × 2.7.	1.9
10	If $a = 4$, $b = 5$, find the value of $(5a + 4b) \div 8$.	5
11	$2(x + 11) = 30$, so x =	4
12	Write down the smallest number that will divide exactly by BOTH 6 and 9.	18

B

ANSWER

		ANSWER
1	£2·10 ÷ 5 =	42p
2	A coat costing £24 is reduced by 20%. How much do I pay?	£ 19·20
3	Change 2055 g to kg.	2.055 kg
4	1.435 m × 6	= 8 m 610 mm
		= 8.610 m
5	In which millennium was the year 1935?	2nd millennium
6	How long will it take to drive 600 km travelling at 80 km/h?	7 h 30 min
7	Find the perimeter of a semicircle of diameter 10 cm. $\pi = 3.14$	25.7 cm
8	The interior angle of each corner of a regular polygon is 135°. How many sides does the polygon have?	8
9	The word MERCHANT is painted on the outside of a glass door. Which letters look the same from the inside of the door?	M, H, A, T
10	Approximate 2888 mℓ to the nearest litre.	3 ℓ

C

ANSWER

The graph shows the number of compact discs sold in one week by a music shop. The average price of a CD sold by the shop is £8·50.

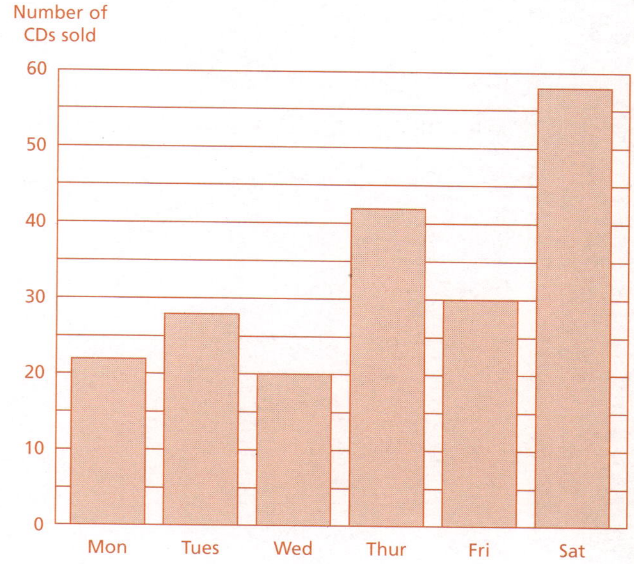

		ANSWER
1	How many CDs were sold on Friday?	30
2	How much money did the shop take from CD sales on Friday?	£ 255
3	Which day had the lowest number of sales?	Wed
4	What was the shop's takings from CDs on that day?	£ 170
5	What was the largest number of CDs sold on one day?	58
6	On which day did sales increase the most as compared with sales on the day before?	Sat
7	What was the total number of CDs sold in the week?	200
8	How much money did the shop take from CDs in the week?	£ 1700
9	What was the mean (average) number of CDs sold each day during the week? (give your answer to the nearest whole one)	33
10	What percentage of the total weekly sales of CDs took place on Saturday?	29%
11	On which day did the shop sell exactly 15% of the weekly total?	Fri
12	What percentage of the total weekly sales took place on the last three days of the week?	65%

Section 1 Test 9

A

ANSWER

1 $1760 - 880 =$ 880

2 $85 \div 15 =$ 5 rem 10

3 $3.06 \times 10^3 =$ 3060

4 Write the following in order of size, smallest first: $\frac{2}{3}$, 23%, 2.3 — 23%, $\frac{2}{3}$, 2.3

5 What is 7.5% of 400? 30

6 $0.5 \times 0.6 =$ 0.3

7 $1.05 + (2.4 \times 1.5) =$ 4.65

8 Approximate 5270 to two significant figures. 5300

9 Work out correct to two significant figures 5.271 + 1.527. 6.8

10 If $m = 7$ and $n = 3$, find the value of $\frac{mn}{m+n}$. 2.1

11 $\frac{x+7}{2} = 10$, so $x =$ 13

12 What is the largest number that will divide exactly into BOTH 24 and 32? 8

B

ANSWER

1 £6·50 ÷ 5 = £ 1·30

2 A jumper costing £8 is reduced by 15%. How much do I save? £ 1·20

3 Change 1470 m to km. 1.470 km

4 6.2 m – 558 cm = 62 cm = 0.62 m

5 In which century was the year 1066? 11th century

6 A train goes at 96 km/h for 35 minutes. How far does it travel? 56 km

7 Find the circumference of a wheel of radius 30 cm. $\pi = 3.14$ — 188.4 cm

8 The smallest angle of a parallelogram is 50°. What size is the largest angle? 130°

9 Which letters of the word CHALK have either a vertical axis of symmetry, or a horizontal axis of symmetry, but NOT both? C, A, K

10 Approximate 188 minutes to the nearest hour. 3 h

C

ANSWER

The Wilson family get a fares list and timetable to plan some coach trips.

FARES Destination	Dep Code	Adult	Child	Return time
Nottingham	D	£4·95	£3·95	1645
Skipton	B	£5·50	£4·80	1800
Whitby	A	£5·85	£4·75	1630
Haworth	C	£4·75	£3·85	1630
York	E	£4·45	£3·95	1600

TIMETABLE	Departure Code				
Pick up Point	A	B	C	D	E
Barnsley	0830	0900	1000	0920	1030
Dewsbury	0850	0950	1050	0830	1050
Doncaster	–	0830	0930	0950	–
Ossett	0900	0940	1040	0840	1100
Wakefield	0910	0930	1030	0850	1110

1 How much will it cost for Mr Wilson to take his two children to York? £ 12·35

2 At what time does the York coach depart from Barnsley? 1030

3 Where does the York coach next pick up after leaving Dewsbury? Ossett

4 At what time is the last pick up point before going on to York? 1110

5 If the coach takes 45 minutes to travel from Wakefield to York, at what time will it arrive at York? 1155

6 At what time does the coach set off from York on its return? 1600

7 How long do passengers have to visit York? 4 h 5 min

8 At what time does the Skipton coach leave Doncaster? 0830

9 Where does the Skipton coach make its last pick up? Dewsbury

10 Where does the Nottingham coach begin its journey? Dewsbury

11 How long after leaving Doncaster does the Haworth coach make its last pick up? 1 h 20 min

12 Grandma Wilson gets a 50p reduction off the adult fare. How much will it cost for herself and her grandson to visit Whitby? £ 10·10

Section 1 Test 10

A

		ANSWER
1	7006 – 6007 =	999
2	(85 × 3) + (7 × 85) =	850
3	$1.7 \times 10^4 =$	17 000
4	Choose one from this list to fill the gap: $1\frac{3}{4}$, 180%, $\frac{17}{10}$	$1.7 < 1\frac{3}{4} < \frac{45}{25}$
5	Write 7.5% of 4 as a decimal.	0.3
6	0.6 ÷ 0.5 =	1.2
7	(2.88 ÷ 1.2) ÷ 1.2 =	2
8	Approximate 3082 to two significant figures.	3100
9	Estimate to the nearest ten 5.04 x 9.88	50
10	If $h = 13$ and $k = 7$, find the value of $(h + k)(h - k)$.	120
11	$a + 5 = 0$, so $a =$	–5
12	Which three of this set of numbers are prime? {1, 2, 5, 9, 15, 21, 23}	2, 5, 23

B

		ANSWER
1	£15·05 ÷ 7 =	£ 2·15
2	A camera costing £85 is reduced by £17. What % saving is this?	20%
3	Change 3.542 tonnes to kg.	3542 kg
4	3.2 t – 1455 kg =	1 t 745 kg
	=	1.745 t
5	If 14.11.1996 was a Thursday, what day was it on 22.11.1996?	Friday
6	How long will it take to travel 600 m at 18 km/h?	2 min
7	Find the area of a circle whose radius is 10 mm. $A = \pi r^2$ $\pi = 3.14$	314 mm^2
8	An isosceles triangle is drawn so that the largest angle equals the sum of the other two angles. How big is the largest angle?	90°
9	The word EXIT is painted on the inside of a glass door. Which letters look the same from the outside of the door?	X, I, T
10	Three TV programmes last 25 min, 55 min and 1 h 35 min respectively. What is the total of all three programmes to the nearest hour?	3 h

C

ANSWER

Mr Akhtar is ordering stock to sell in his computer shop. The prices shown do not include Value Added Tax (VAT) at 17.5%.

COMPUTERS	LESS V.A.T.
Basic model	£600·00
Multimedia	£1400·00
Portable	£1000·00
PRINTERS	
Dot matrix	£100·00
Ink jet	£200·00
Laser	£400·00
MONITORS	
14 inch	£150·00
17 inch	£350·00
ACCESSORIES	
Disks (per ten)	£2·50
Disk box	£5·00
Spare mouse	£18·00

		ANSWER
1	How much VAT must be added to the cost of a portable computer?	£ 175
2	What is the VAT on a basic model computer?	£ 105
3	What is the cost of a laser printer including VAT?	£ 470
4	What will it cost Mr Akhtar to order three basic model computers and two portables, including VAT?	£ 4465
5	What is the cost of ordering 200 disks and 10 disk boxes, including VAT?	£ 117·50
6	What is the VAT inclusive cost of two 14 inch monitors and an ink jet printer?	£ 587·50

When Mr Akhtar sells his goods he adds a further 20% profit to the VAT inclusive price he paid to the supplier.

		ANSWER
7	What profit is added to the cost of a laser printer?	£ 94
8	What is the selling price of a laser printer, including profit?	£ 564
9	What profit does Mr Akhtar make by selling a dot matrix printer?	£ 23·50
10	What is the selling price of a multimedia computer?	£ 1974
11	What is the profit on a portable computer with an ink jet printer?	£ 282
12	What is the selling price of a spare mouse?	£ 25·38

Section 1 Test 11

A

		ANSWER
1	$1760 \times 11 =$	19 360
2	$155 \div (15 - 5) =$	15 rem 5
3	$2.05 \times 10^2 =$	205
4	Write $\frac{49}{3}$ as a mixed number.	$16\frac{1}{3}$
5	Write $\frac{3}{20}$ of 5 as a decimal.	0.75
6	$20 \div 0.2 =$	100
7	$(6.3 \times 1.7) + (0.3 \times 6.3) =$	12.6
8	Approximate 3.082 to two significant figures.	3.1
9	Estimate to the nearest ten 16.048×5.101.	80
10	If $p = 2.5$ and $q = 0.5$, find the value of $\frac{p}{q}$.	5
11	$2x + 3x = 15$, so $x =$	3
12	Write down the prime factors of 30 (i.e. those prime numbers which will divide exactly into 30).	2 , 3 , 5

B

		ANSWER
1	£3·45 × 6 =	£ 20·70
2	I buy a plate for £2·60 and sell it for £3·20. What is my profit?	60p
3	Change $2\frac{1}{2}$ km to m.	2500 m
4	2.5ℓ – 955 mℓ	= 1ℓ 545 mℓ = 1.545 ℓ
5	If 23.06.1997 was a Monday, what date will it be on Thursday of the following week?	03.07.1997
6	Find the distance travelled in 2 minutes at a rate of 16 m/s.	1.92 km
7	Find the diameter of a circle whose circumference is 157 mm. $\pi = 3.14$	50 mm
8	A circle passes through each corner of a right-angled triangle whose longest side is 10 cm. What size is the diameter of the circle?	10 cm
9	Which letter of the word LAUGH has an axis of symmetry which is neither vertical nor horizontal?	L
10	If two dozen pencils cost £1·95 find the cost of one pencil to the nearest penny.	8p

C

ANSWER

Sairah and Jamie are playing a game with two dice and a coin. First they throw the dice and note down the numbers. Then they toss the coin. If the coin falls heads they add the two numbers from the dice. If the coin falls tails they multiply together the numbers from the dice. For example, throws of 3 and 2 on the dice will give a score of 3 + 2 = 5 if the coin falls heads and 3 × 2 = 6 if the coin falls tails. The first two lines of the table show more examples. Now fill in the blanks on the other lines.

	THROW 1	THROW 2	HEADS	TAILS
	2	5	7	10
	1	1	2	1
1	6	1	7	6
2	4	2	6	8
3	3	6	9	18
4	5	4	9	20
5	2	6	8	12
6	6	6	12	36
7	5	5	10	25
8	2	2	4	4
9	4	4	8	16

10	What is the largest score that can be made?	36
11	What is the largest possible score if the coin falls heads?	12
12	If they had another go and the score was 15, how did the coin fall, heads or tails?	tails

Section 1 Test 12

A

		ANSWER
1	$1760 \div 16 =$	110
2	$(0 + 5) \times (5 - 5) =$	0
3	$3.17 \times 10^3 =$	3170
4	Put the following in order of size, smallest first: $1\frac{1}{2}$, 0.5, 1.5%, $\frac{15}{50}$.	1.5%, $\frac{15}{50}$, 0.5, $1\frac{1}{2}$
5	Express 15% of 3 as a fraction in its lowest terms.	$\frac{9}{20}$
6	$2 - 0.008 + 1.4 =$	3.392
7	$(2.2 \times 4.5) - (1.5 \times 2.2) =$	6.6
8	Approximate 1.057 to two significant figures.	1.1
9	Estimate to the nearest ten $2480 \div 49$	50
10	If $x = 2$, $y = 3$, $z = 5$, find the value of $(xy + yz) \div (x + y + z)$.	2.1
11	$3p - 5 = p + 1$, so $p =$	3
12	Write down the next two numbers of the sequence 1, 3, 7, 15, ___, ___	31, 63

B

		ANSWER
1	£100 ÷ 80 =	£ 1·25
2	I put down 10% deposit on a car costing £8750. How much is left to pay?	£ 7875
3	Change 3.3 m to mm.	3300 mm
4	3.75 m + 452 cm + 1105 mm =	9.375 m
5	The time 11.35 is the same as ___ minutes to ___	25 minutes to 12
6	Change 1m/s to km/h.	3.6 km/h
7	Find the area of a square field whose perimeter is 60 m.	225 m^2
8	A rhombus is drawn so that its smallest angle is half the size of its largest angle. What size is the smallest angle?	60°
9	Which letters of the word BOUGHT have both a vertical and a horizontal axis of symmetry?	O, H
10	If 1000 articles cost £27, find the cost of one to the nearest penny.	3p

C

Debbie and Charlie play a game with spinners.

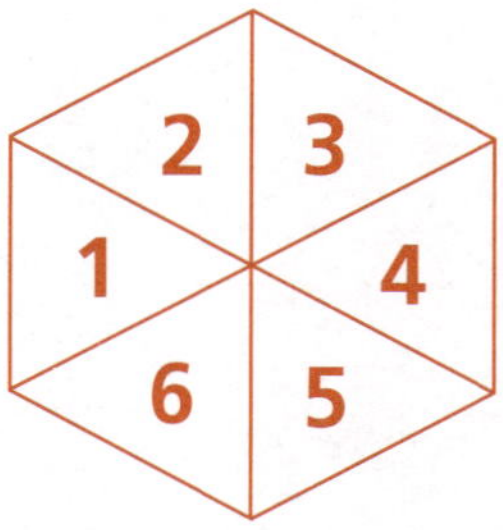

Debbie's Spinner

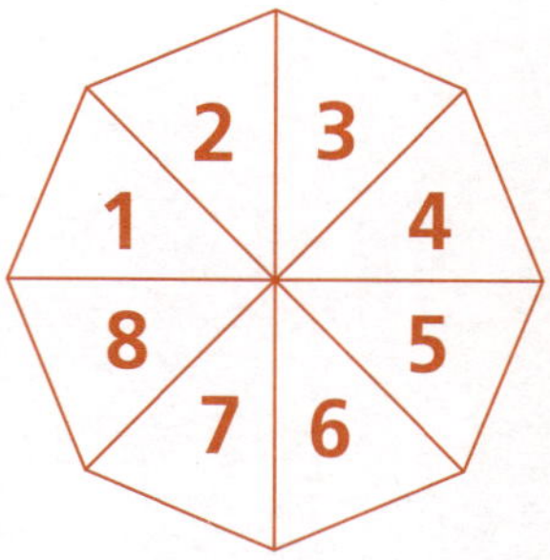

Charlie's Spinner

Express your answers as fractions in their lowest terms.

		ANSWER
1	What is the probability of Debbie spinning a 6?	$\frac{1}{6}$
2	What is the probability of Charlie spinning a 6?	$\frac{1}{8}$
3	What is the probability of Debbie NOT spinning a 6?	$\frac{5}{6}$
4	What is the probability of Charlie NOT spinning an 8?	$\frac{7}{8}$
5	What is the probability of Debbie spinning an odd number?	$\frac{1}{2}$
6	What is the probability of Charlie NOT spinning an odd number?	$\frac{1}{2}$
7	What is the probability of Debbie spinning EITHER a 5 OR a 6?	$\frac{1}{3}$
8	What is the probability of Debbie spinning a number greater than 4?	$\frac{1}{3}$
9	What is the probability of Charlie spinning a number greater than 4?	$\frac{1}{2}$
10	What is the probability of Charlie spinning a number less than 4?	$\frac{3}{8}$
11	What is the probability of Charlie spinning EITHER a number greater than 4 OR a number less than 4?	$\frac{7}{8}$

12 Explain why the answer to question 11 is less than 1.

Because it does not include the probability of spinning exactly 4.

Section 1 Revision Test

		ANSWER
1	$128 + 281 + 812 =$	1221
2	$(156 - 65) \div 7 =$	13
3	$3.01 \times 10^2 =$	301
4	Express 350% as a mixed number.	$3\frac{1}{2}$
5	Write 8% of 30 as a decimal.	2.4
6	$0.04 - 2 + 1.98 =$	0.02
7	$(3.2 - 2.3) \times (3.2 + 2.3) =$	4.95
8	Approximate 3.066 to two significant figures.	3.1
9	Calculate 2.995×4.037 correct to two significant figures.	12
10	If $a = 3$, $b = 4$, find the value of $a^2 + 2ab$.	33
11	$3p + 5 = p + 9$, so $p =$	2
12	$\sqrt{121} =$	11
13	£3·55 × 5 =	£ 17·75
14	A pair of shoes costing £23·50 is reduced by 10% in a sale. How much do I save?	£ 2·35
15	Change 63.63 cm to mm.	636.3 mm
16	1.72 kg + 5280 g =	7 kg
17	If the 25th of January is a Friday, what day will it be on February 8th?	Friday
18	A train goes at 72 km/h for 20 minutes. How far does it travel?	24 km
19	A wheel travels 125.6 m in 20 revolutions. What is its diameter? $\boxed{\pi = 3.14}$	2 m
20	The interior angle of each corner of a regular polygon is 90°. How many sides does the polygon have?	4
21	Which letters of the words POST OFFICE have one, and only one, axis of symmetry?	T C E
22	If a dozen exercise books cost £5·95, find the cost of one book to the nearest penny.	50p
23	The coordinates of three of the corners of a square are (0, 0), (0, 5), (5, 5). What are the coordinates of the other corner?	(5 , 0)
24	How many tiles 200 mm square are needed to cover a wall measuring 3 m by 2.4 m?	180
25	What is the possibility of throwing EITHER a 2 or a number greater than 4 on a six-sided die?	$\frac{1}{2}$

Section 1 Revision Test

ANSWER

Kerry is helping her mother with their market stall. They buy plants from the wholesaler and re-sell them on the stall. Kerry uses a spreadsheet to look after their accounts.

	A	B	C	D	E	F	G	H	I
1	Name of	Buying	Number	Spending	Selling	Number	Income	Number	Value
2	Plant	Price	bought	on plants	price	sold	from plants	unsold	unsold
3	Buddleia	£2·71	15	£40·65	£3·25	4	£13·00	11	£35·75
4	Clematis	£3·75	12	£45·00	£4·50	6	£27·00	6	£27·00
5	Fuchsia	£0·79	65	£51·35	£0·95	33	£31·35	32	£30·40
6	Heather	£1·00	36	£36·00	£1·20	26	£31·20	10	£12·00
7	Hebe	£1·58	25	£39·50	£1·90	14	£26·60	11	£20·90
8	Hosta	£1·25	24	£30·00	£1·50	8	£12·00	16	£24·00
9	Lavender	£1·37	30	£41·10	£1·65	19	£31·35	11	£18·15
10	Potentilla	£2·37	12	£28·44	£2·85	7	£19·95	5	£14·25
11	Pyracantha	£2·08	10	£20·80	£2·50	8	£20·00	2	£5·00
12	Viburnum	£6·00	6	£36·00	£7·20	2	£14·40	4	£28·80
13			235	£368·84		127	£226·85	108	£216·25

26 What total number of plants do Kerry and her mother buy? — 235

27 What total amount do they spend in buying the plants? — £ 368·84

28 What total number of plants do they sell on the stall? — 127

29 What is their total income from selling plants? — £ 226·85

30 What total number of plants are left unsold? — 108

31 What is the total value of the unsold plants? — £ 216·25

32 What is the most expensive plant they have for sale? — Viburnum

33 Which plant do they buy most of? — Fuchsia

34 Which plant do they sell least of? — Viburnum

35 Which two plants bring in most income? — Fuchsia , Lavender

36 What is the buying price of a Heather plant? — £ 1·00

37 What profit is made from selling each Heather plant? — £ 0·20

38 What decimal fraction of the buying price is this profit? — 0.2

39 What percentage profit is made from selling Viburnum? — 20%

The formula used to calculate the total number of plants bought is SUM(C3:C12)

40 What formula is used to find the total number of plants sold? — SUM(F3:F12)

41 What formula is used to find the total income from plant sales? — SUM(G3:G12)

The formula used to find the spending on Heather is B6*C6, where * means 'multiply'.

42 What formula is used to find the income from Heather plants? — E6*F6

43 What formula is used to find the income from Hosta plants? — E8*F8

The formula used to find the selling price of a Heather plant is B6 + (B6*0.2).

44 What formula is used to find the selling price of Viburnum? — B12 + (B12*0.2)

45 What formula could be used to find the selling price of Clematis if they had wanted to make 25% profit? — B4 + (B4*0.25)

Mental Arithmetic 6

Name of student …………………………………		**Diagnostic Chart for Section 2** Indicate where the student has difficulty											
		1	2	3	4	5	6	7	8	9	10	11	12
Test 1	Part A												
	Part B												
	Part C												
Test 2	Part A												
	Part B												
	Part C												
Test 3	Part A												
	Part B												
	Part C												
Test 4	Part A												
	Part B												
	Part C												
Test 5	Part A												
	Part B												
	Part C												
Test 6	Part A												
	Part B												
	Part C												
Test 7	Part A												
	Part B												
	Part C												
Test 8	Part A												
	Part B												
	Part C												
Test 9	Part A												
	Part B												
	Part C												
Test 10	Part A												
	Part B												
	Part C												
Test 11	Part A												
	Part B												
	Part C												
Test 12	Part A												
	Part B												
	Part C												

Section 2 Test 1

A

		ANSWER
1	Write down the product of 15 and 25.	375
2	(84 + 66) ÷ 30 =	5
3	Write in figures 2.57 million.	2 570 000
4	Express the ratio 4:5 as a percentage.	80%
5	Increase 20 by 20%.	24
6	0.083 + 3.08 =	3.163
7	(1.25 × 5) – (1.25 ÷ 5) =	6
8	Approximate 1.603 to (a) 2 decimal places, (b) 2 significant figures.	 (a) 1·60 (b) 1·6
9	Estimate to the nearest ten 28.6 × 3.22	90
10	If $x = 2$, $y = 3$, $z = 5$, evaluate $5x + 3y - 2z$.	9
11	$10x + 10 = 100$, so x =	9
12	What is the smallest number that is exactly divisible by BOTH 6 and 8?	24

B

		ANSWER
1	How many articles costing 40p each can I buy for £12?	30
2	A blouse at £10·50 is reduced by $33\frac{1}{3}$% How much do I pay?	£ 7
3	$28\frac{1}{2}$ in =	2 ft $4\frac{1}{2}$ in
4	65 in + 115 in =	180 in = 15 ft = 5 yd
5	A TV programme lasts $1\frac{1}{4}$ hours. It begins at 6.50 pm. At what time does it finish?	8.05 pm
6	If 1ℓ of water has a mass of 1 kg, what is its density in g/cm³? Note: 1ℓ = 1000 cm³	1 g/cm³
7	Find the perimeter of a rectangular room 2.8 m wide and 3.5 m long.	12.6 m
8	Use Pythagoras' Theorem to find the length of side x. 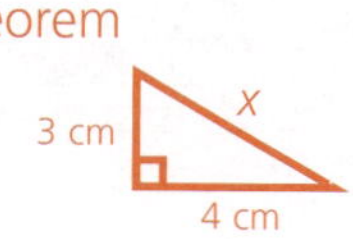	5 cm
9	What is the number of axes of symmetry of a square? 	4
10	Find 20% of £14·99 to the nearest £1.	£ 3

C

ANSWER

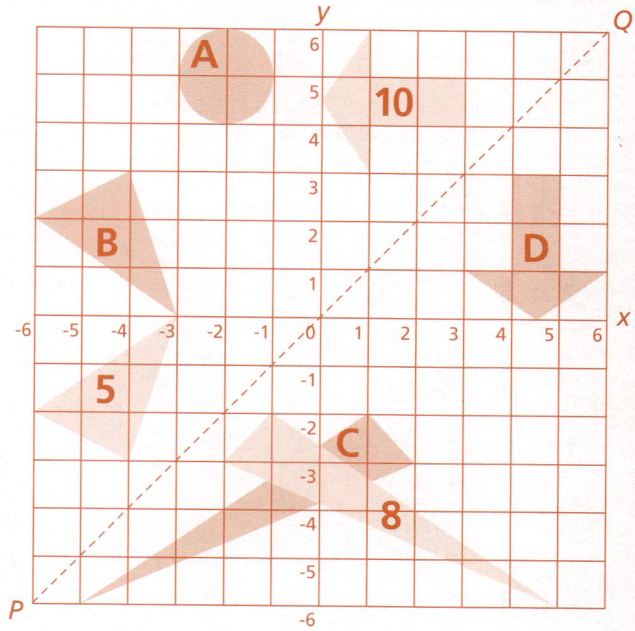

1	Write down the coordinates of the centre of circle A.	(–2 , 5)
2	Write down the coordinates of the centre of the reflection of circle A in the y-axis.	(2 , 5)
3	Write down the coordinates of the centre of the reflection of circle A in the x-axis.	(–2 , –5)
4	Write down the coordinates of the corners of triangle B.	(–3 , 0)(–4 , 3)(–6 , 2)
5	On the grid above, sketch in the position of the reflection of triangle B in the x-axis.	
6	Write down the coordinates of each corner of the reflection of triangle B in the x-axis.	(–3 , 0)(–4 , –3)(–6 , –2)
7	Write down the coordinates of the corners of triangle C.	(1 , –2)(2 , –3)(–5 , –6)
8	On the grid above, sketch in the reflection of triangle C in the y-axis.	
9	Write down the coordinates of the corners of the reflection of triangle C in the y-axis.	(–1 , –2)(–2 , –3)(5 , –6)
10	On the grid above, sketch in the reflection of object D about the diagonal line PQ.	

Here are four statements describing changes that could occur when an object undergoes a reflection:

A The x-values of its coordinates stay unaltered and the y-values change sign (from +ve to –ve or from –ve to +ve).

B The y-values of its coordinates stay unaltered and the x-values change sign.

C Both the x-values and the y-values of its coordinates change sign.

D The x-values become the y-values and the y-values become the x-values.

11	Which statement A, B, C or D correctly describes a reflection in the x-axis?	A
12	Which statement A, B, C or D correctly describes a reflection in the y-axis?	B

Section 2 Test 2

A

ANSWER

1. 500 000 + 500 + 5 = **500 505**
2. Write down (a) the quotient and (b) the remainder when 56 is divided by 9. (a) **6** (b) **2**
3. Express 2 × 2 × 2 × 2 × 2 in index notation. **2^5**
4. Express 0.25 as a ratio in its lowest terms. **1:4**
5. What is $\frac{2}{5}$ of 40? **16**
6. 0.05 x 45 = **2.25**
7. (1.25 × 5) ÷ (1.25 ÷ 5) = **25**
8. Approximate 112.345 to (a) 2 decimal places, (a) **112.35** (b) 2 significant figures. (b) **110.00**
9. Estimate to the nearest ten $\frac{305 \times 21}{44}$ **150**
10. If $a = 3$, $b = 5$, evaluate $a^2 + b$. **14**
11. $\frac{t + 2}{5} = 4$, so $t =$ **18**
12. Express 30 as a product of prime numbers by filling in the blanks. **2** × **3** × **5** = 30

B

ANSWER

1. How many articles costing 30p each can I buy for £10·50? **35**
2. I buy a table for £120 with 8 equal instalments. How much is each payment? £ **15**
3. 35 oz = **2 lb 3 oz**
4. 3 ft 6 in – 30 in = **12 in = 1 ft**
5. The 11.17 train to London arrives at 14.03. How long does the journey take? **2 h 46 min**
6. If 1 ℓ of oil has a mass of 800 g, what is its density in g/cm³? **0.8 g/cm³**
7. A glass sheet 6 mm thick measures 110 cm by 40 cm. Find its volume in cm³. **2640 cm³**
8. Write down the length of side x. **50 cm**

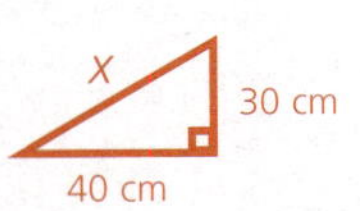

9. A box has a square lid. In how many ways can the lid be turned so that it still fits the box? **4**

10. Approximate 2940 m to the nearest km. **3 km**

C

ANSWER

Kelly has five large photographs she wants to mount and frame. Each photograph measures 400 mm by 300 mm and is stuck onto a piece of mounting card measuring 500 mm by 400 mm. The mounting card and photo will then be placed under glass in a wooden frame.

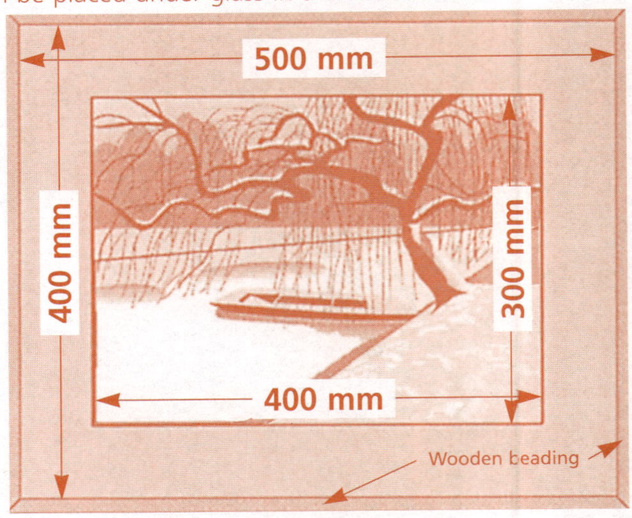

1. What is the size in metres of each piece of mounting card? **0.5** m by **0.4** m
2. What is the area in m² of each piece of mounting card? **0.2 m²**
3. Each photo is stuck to the middle of the mounting card so as to give a border of equal width on all four sides. How many mm wide is this border? **50 mm**
4. How many pieces of mounting card can be cut from a full sheet measuring 841 mm by 594 mm? **2**
5. How many full sheets of card will Kelly need to buy in order to mount all five photos? **3**
6. If a full sheet of card costs £2·35 how much will it cost Kelly to buy enough full sheets for all five photos? £ **7·05**
7. Kelly orders some glass the same size as each piece of mounting card. What is the area in m² of each piece of glass? **0.2 m²**
8. If glass costs £11·20 per m² how much will each piece cost? £ **2·24**
9. How much will it cost to buy the glass for all five photos? £ **11·20**
10. What length of wooden beading will be needed to make each frame? Add on 10% extra for wastage. **1.98 m**
11. The beading costs £3·15 per 2 metre length. How much will it cost to buy enough beading for all five frames? £ **15·75**
12. What is the total cost for Kelly to frame all five photos? £ **34·00**

Section 2 Test 3

A

ANSWER

1 $243 \div 27 =$ 9

2 $24 - (15 - 3) =$ 12

3 $11.01 \times 10^2 =$ 1101

4 Express $1\frac{1}{2}$ as a percentage. 150%

5 What is 150% of 3? 4.5

6 $2.56 \div 1.6 =$ 1.6

7 $(1.25 + 5) + (1.25 \times 5) =$ 12.5

8 Approximate 69.802 to
(a) 2 decimal places (a) 69.80

(b) 2 significant figures. (b) 70

9 Estimate to the nearest 100
$6358 \div 7.8$. 800

10 If $a = 2$, $t = 5$, evaluate at^2. 50

11 $5q - 40 = 0$, so $q =$ 8

12 Express 28 as a product of prime numbers by filling in the blanks.
$2 \times 2 \times 7 = 28$

B

ANSWER

1 If 10 articles cost £2·40, then 1 will cost 24 p

2 How long will it take to pay £27·50 at £2·50 per week? 11 weeks

3 40 pints = 5 gallons

4 6 ft 6 in x 10 = 65 ft = 21 yd 2 ft

5 Pythagoras died in 497 BC aged 85. In what year was he born? 582 BC

6 1 kg of sand has a volume of 400 cm^3. What is its density in g/cm^3? 2.5 g/cm^3

7 A box is 0.5 m wide, 0.8 m long and 0.35 m high. Find its volume. 0.14 m^3

8 Write down the length of side x.

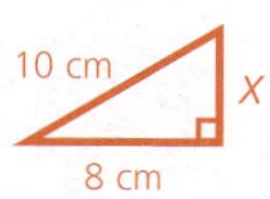

$x =$ 6 cm

9 A cardboard square has its outline marked on a sheet of paper. What is the smallest angle of rotation of the square about its centre O that will bring it back onto its outline again?

90 °

10 Approximate 20 ft to the nearest yard. 7 yd

C

ANSWER

The table below is part of a spreadsheet that Patrick used to calculate the squares and cubes of the numbers 1 to 10. Some of the values in the table are missing.

	A	B	C
1	Number	Square	Cube
2	1	1	1
3	2	4	8
4	3	9	27
5	4	16	64
6	5	25	125
7	6	36	216
8	7	49	343
9	8	64	512
10	9	81	729
11	10	100	1000
12	Total	385	3025

1 What is the content of cell B5? 16

2 What is the content of cell C11? 1000

3 What is the content of cell A1? Number

4 What number is missing from cell A6? 5

5 What number is missing from cell C6? 125

6 What number is missing from cell C4? 27

7 What number is missing from cell B9? 64

8 The value of cell B7 was found by using the formula A7*A7.

What formula was used to calculate the value of cell B10? A10*A10

9 The value of cell C7 can be found by using the formula A7*A7*A7.

What formula can be used to calculate the cube of 9? A10*A10*A10

11 What would be the result of using the formula A10*B10? 729

10 The value of cell C12 was found by using the formula SUM(C2:C11).

What would be the result of using the formula SUM(B2:B11)? 385

12 What number is missing from cell B12? 385

Section 2 Test 4

A

		ANSWER
1	1000 – 587 + 113	526
2	24 ÷ (15 – 3) =	2
3	Write in figures 10^6.	1 000 000
4	Write in order of size, starting with the smallest: 2:3, 2.3, 23%, $\frac{3}{2}$.	23% , 2:3 , $\frac{3}{2}$, 2.3
5	Divide 30 in the ratio 2:3.	12 : 18
6	0.6 × 0.3 =	0.18
7	$\frac{5.4}{1.8 \times 0.5} =$	6
8	Approximate 0.3572 to (a) 2 decimal places	(a) 0.36
	(b) 2 significant figures.	(b) 0.36
9	Estimate $\frac{5964}{14.5 \times 4.1}$ to the nearest 100.	100
10	If $x = 3$, $y = 4$, evaluate $2x + y^2$	22
11	$4a - 20 = 2a$, so $a =$	10
12	$6^3 =$	216

B

		ANSWER
1	What is the change from £1 if I buy 3 articles at 18p each?	46p
2	How many Austrian schillings for £50 at 16 schillings to £1?	800
3	3 ft 6 in =	42 in
4	15 yd – 12 ft =	33 ft = 11 yd
5	How many days inclusive from 14th March to 3rd May?	51 days
6	The density of water is 1 g/cm³. What is this in kg/m³?	1000 kg/m³
7	A wooden block measures 3 cm × 4 cm × 5 cm. Find its total surface area.	94 cm²
8	Write down the length of side x.	20 cm
9	A cardboard square has its outline marked on a sheet of paper. How many times can the square be rotated 90° about its centre to bring it back onto its outline again?	4
10	Approximate 2444 kg to the nearest tonne.	2 t

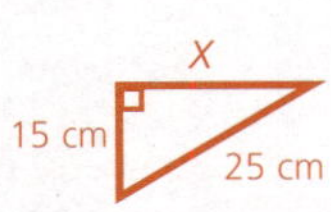

C

ANSWER

The diagram shows a plot of land with a house and garden. The grid lines are spaced 1 cm apart.

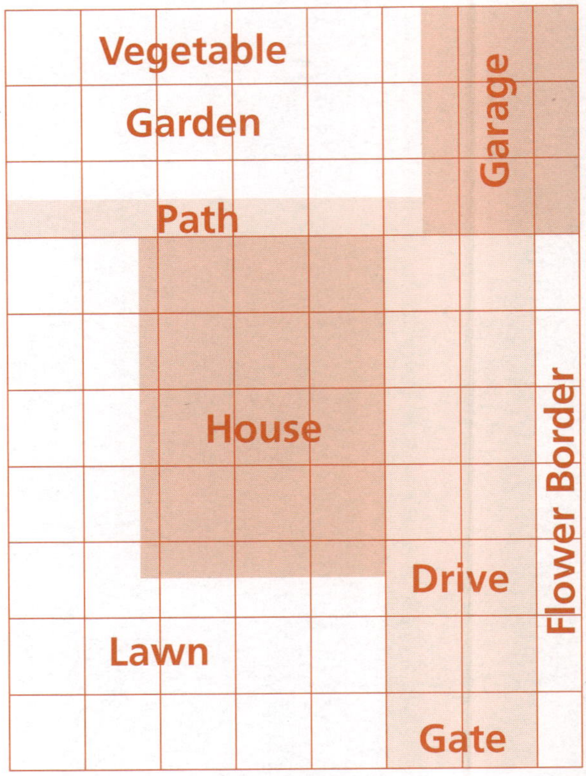

Scale 1 : 200

		ANSWER
1	What length in metres is represented by 1 cm on the plan?	2 m
2	What size is the drive?	4 m by 14 m
3	What is the area of the drive?	56 m²
4	Which has the bigger area, the drive or the vegetable garden, and by how much?	Drive by 1 m²
5	What length of fencing is needed to go all round the plot, not including the gate?	66 m
6	What is the total area of the plot?	300 m²
7	What is the area of the garage?	24 m²
8	What percentage of the plot is occupied by the garage?	8 %
9	What is the area of the house?	58.5 m²
10	What percentage of the plot is occupied by the house?	19.5 %
11	What is the area of the lawn?	81.5 m²
12	How many stone slabs 500 mm square will be needed to pave the path?	44

Section 2 Test 5

A

ANSWER

			Answer
1	$587 - 1000 + 643 =$		230
2	$24 \div (15 \div 3) =$		4 rem 4
3	Write in figures 3.5×10^5		350 000
4	Express $\frac{9}{25}$ as (a) a decimal,	(a)	0.36
	(b) a percentage and	(b)	36%
	(c) a ratio in its lowest terms.	(c)	9 : 25
5	Reduce 90 by 15%.		76.5
6	$0.3 \div 0.6 =$		0.5
7	$\frac{5.4 \times 0.5}{1.8} =$		1.5
8	Approximate 0.0772 to (a) 2 decimal places,	(a)	0.08
	(b) 2 significant figures.	(b)	0.077
9	Calculate $52 \div 6$ correct to two decimal places.		8.67
10	If $m = 6$, $n = 5$, evaluate $m^2 - n^2$.		11
11	$\frac{1}{2}(3 + x) = 4$,	so $x =$	5
12	$\sqrt{49} =$		7

B

ANSWER

		Answer
1	I buy magazines costing £1·35, £2·20 and 85p. How much change from £5?	60p
2	How much will 500 German marks cost at 2.5 marks to £1?	£ 200
3	5 lb 6 oz =	86 oz
4	3 lb 12 oz + 4 lb 8 oz =	8 lb 4 oz
5	How many hours and minutes between 8.46 am and 3.22 pm?	6 h 36 min
6	1 m^3 of olive oil has a mass of 920 kg. What is the volume of 460 g of oil?	500 cm^3
7	A tank 0.75 m tall has a square base of side 0.8 m. Find its volume.	0.48 m^3
8	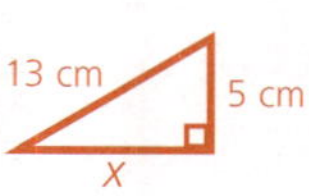 Use Pythagoras' Theorem to find the length of side x.	12 cm
9	What is the order of rotational symmetry of a square about its centre. 	4
10	Approximate 145 lb to the nearest stone.	10 stone

C

ANSWER

The graph shows the land area of ten National Parks.

Area in sq km

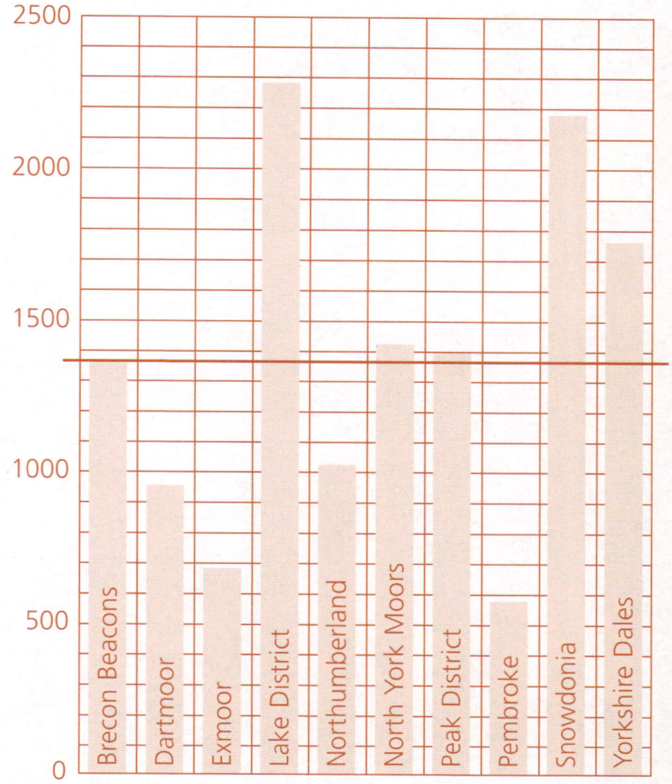

		Answer
1	Which is the smallest National Park?	Pembroke
2	Which is the largest National Park?	Lake District
3	Which Park is approximately half the area of Northumberland?	Pembroke
4	The largest Park is approximately how many times bigger than the smallest Park?	4
5	Estimate the total area of all ten Parks? (to nearest 100 km^2).	13 600 km^2
6	Estimate the mean (average) area of the ten Parks.	1360 km^2
7	Draw a line on the graph to show the mean area of the Parks.	
8	Which Park is nearest in area to the mean?	Brecon Beacons
9	The Brecon Beacons is approximately what percentage of the total area?	10%
10	Which park is approximately 5% of the total area?	Exmoor
11	Which Park is approximately one-eighth of the total area?	Yorkshire Dales
12	The Lake District is approximately what fraction of the total area?	$\frac{1}{6}$

Section 2 Test 6

A — ANSWER

		ANSWER
1	$221 \div 17 =$	13
2	$24 - (15 \times 3) =$	−21
3	Write in figures 3^4.	81
4	Express the ratio 12:40 (a) as a fraction in its lowest terms,	(a) $\frac{3}{10}$
	(b) as a decimal	(b) 0.3
	(c) as a percentage.	(c) 30%
5	Express $51 \div 8$ as a mixed number.	$6\frac{3}{8}$
6	$5.02 - 0.502 =$	4.518
7	$2\left(\frac{3.6 + 4.8}{0.6}\right) =$	28
8	Approximate 0.00822 to (a) 2 decimal places	(a) 0.01
	(b) 2 significant figures.	(b) 0.0082
9	Estimate correct to one significant figure $(9.973 + 5.032) \div 2.986$.	5
10	If $m = 6$, $n = 5$, evaluate $(m + n)(m - n)$	11
11	$\frac{3}{p} = \frac{1}{3}$, so $p =$	9
12	Write in the next two terms of the sequence 1, 3, 6, 10,	15, 21

B — ANSWER

		ANSWER
1	How much change from £10 if I spend £2·45, £1·80 and £3·75?	£ 2
2	What must I sell a £60 table for to make a profit of 30%?	£ 78
3	$2\frac{1}{2}$ gallons =	20 pints
4	5 lb 2 oz − 3 lb 10 oz =	1 lb 8 oz
5	How many hours and minutes from 7.30 p.m. Friday to 11.15 a.m. Monday?	63 h 45 min
6	80 g of dry cleaning fluid has a volume of 50 cm^3. What is the mass of 1 ℓ of fluid?	1.6 kg
7	A wooden cube has a volume of 125 cm^3. How long is the cube's edge?	5 cm
8	Use Pythagoras' Theorem to find the length of side x.	8 m
9	What is the number of axes of symmetry of a rectangle?	2
10	Approximate $2\frac{1}{4}$ million square metres to the nearest square kilometre.	2 km^2

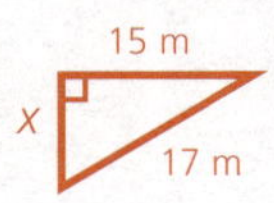

C — ANSWER

Joe and Sidrah are baking cakes. Some of their recipes give quantities in cups and some in grams. They measure out five cups of flour and find that it weighs 800 g. They plot a graph to convert from cups to grams.

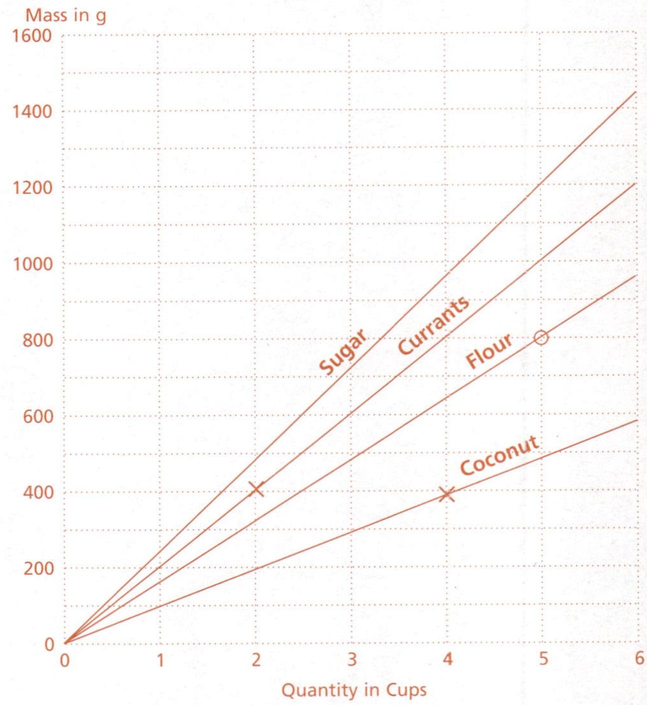

Use the graph to answer the following questions.

		ANSWER
1	What is the mass of 1 cup of flour?	160 g
2	What is the mass of $2\frac{1}{2}$ cups of flour?	400 g
3	About how many cups of flour weigh 0.5 kg?	3

Joe and Sidrah plot a conversion graph for sugar.

		ANSWER
4	What is the mass of 5 cups of sugar?	1200 g
5	About how many cups are needed for 1 kg of sugar?	4
6	Estimate the total mass of 1 cup of sugar and 2 cups of flour.	560 g
7	How many times heavier is sugar than flour? (Hint: compare the mass of 1 cup of sugar with 1 cup of flour)	$1\frac{1}{2}$

Joe and Sidrah find that four cups of coconut weigh 380 g and two cups of currants weigh 400 g.

		ANSWER
8	Plot these two points on the graph above.	
9	Draw conversion graphs for coconut and for currants.	
10	About how many cups of currants weigh the same as 5 cups of flour?	4
11	About how many cups are needed for $\frac{1}{2}$ kg of coconut?	5

A cake recipe needs 3 cups of flour, 1 cup of sugar and $1\frac{1}{2}$ cups of currants.

		ANSWER
12	Estimate the mass of all these ingredients.	1 kg

Section 2 Test 7

A

ANSWER

1 Write down the quotient when 105 is divided by 7. 15

2 $(80 \times 5) - (80 \div 5) =$ 384

3 Express 2047 in standard notation. 2.047×10^3

4 Insert one of the symbols <, >, = to make this statement correct. 36% $<$ $\frac{3}{8}$

5 $1\frac{1}{2} + \frac{5}{8} =$ $2\frac{1}{8}$

6 $1.5 - 2.3 =$ -0.8

7 $3.6 - (1.8 - 0.6) =$ 2.4

8 Approximate 79 256 to 3 significant figures. 79 300

9 Give the answer to (0.07 x 0.08) correct to three decimal places. 0.006

10 If $x = 4$, $y = 2$, $z = 0$, evaluate $\frac{xy + z}{y}$. 4

11 $2 + a = 0$, so $a =$ -2

12 Write in the next two terms of the sequence. 2 , 3 , 5 , 7 , 11 , 13 , 17

B

ANSWER

1 If 8 articles cost £1·76 then 1 will cost 22p

2 I get 60% discount off an insurance premium of £240. How much do I pay? £ 96

3 66 ft = 22 yd

4 $1\frac{1}{2}$ gallons + 10 pints = 2 gallons 6 pints

5 George can swim a length in 19.36 seconds. Jim takes $\frac{3}{10}$ second longer. What is Jim's time? 19.66 s

6 If the density of wood is 600 kg/m^3 what is the volume of a 3 tonne tree? 5 m^3

7 A 10 cm square sheet of metal has a 5 cm square hole cut into it. What area of metal remains? 75 cm^3

8 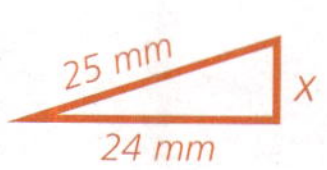

Use Pythagoras' Theorem to find the length of side x. 7 mm

9 A box has a rectangular lid. In how many ways can the lid be turned so that it still fits the box?
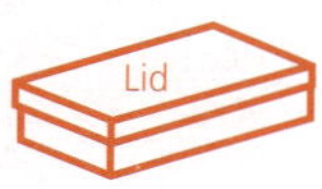

2

10 A box measures 1.92 m long by 1.05 m wide and is 0.55 m deep. Find its approximate volume to the nearest cubic metre. 1 m^3

C

ANSWER

The graphs show annual weather data for Moscow. The bars represent the total monthly rainfall in mm. The line shows the maximum monthly temperature in °C.

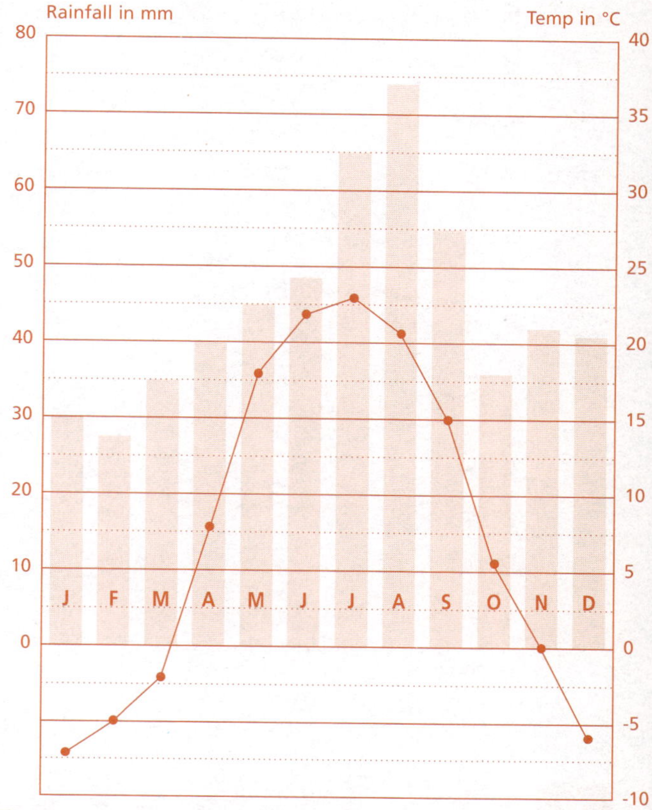

1 Which is the wettest month in Moscow? August

2 Which is Moscow's driest month? February

3 Which is the hottest month in Moscow? July

4 Which is Moscow's coldest month? January

5 During which five months is the maximum temperature at or below 0°C? Nov , Dec , Jan , Feb , Mar

6 Which season (Winter, Spring, Summer or Autumn) is the driest? Winter

7 Which season of the year is the wettest? Summer

8 What is the total rainfall for the wettest three-month period? 194 mm

9 What is the mean (average) rainfall for these three months? (answer to nearest mm) 65 mm

10 What is the mean (average) temperature over the hottest three-month period? (answer to nearest 1°C) 22 °C

11 What is the mean (average) temperature over the first four months of the year? (answer to nearest 0.5°C) −1.5 °C

12 What is the mean (average) temperature over the five wettest months of the year? (answer to nearest 1°C) 20 °C

Section 2 Test 8

A

		ANSWER
1	$-16 + 20 - 4 =$	0
2	$(80 \times 5) - (80 - 5) =$	325
3	Express 204.7 in standard notation.	2.047×10^2
4	9:25 > 0.36 TRUE or FALSE?	FALSE
5	$\frac{3}{10} + \frac{4}{5} =$	$1\frac{1}{10}$
6	$1.2 \times 0.12 =$	0.144
7	$5.5 - \frac{5.5}{2.75 \times 0.5} =$	1.5
8	Approximate 3.008 to 3 significant figures.	3.01
9	Give the answer correct to two decimal places $(0.08)^2 =$	0.01
10	If $a = 4$, $b = 8$, evaluate $\frac{a}{a+b}$ as a fraction in its lowest terms.	$\frac{1}{3}$
11	$5x + 5 = 5$, so $x =$	0
12	Write down the largest number which is an exact divisor of BOTH 32 and 40.	8

B

		ANSWER
1	If 5 articles cost 45p, what will 40 cost?	£ 3·60
2	What is the interest at $8\frac{1}{2}$ % on £1600?	£ 136
3	$5\frac{1}{2}$ yd =	16 ft 6 in
4	$\frac{1}{4}$ mile =	440 yd
5	In which millennium is the year 2010?	3rd millennium
6	How far does an aeroplane flying at 720 km/h travel in 65 minutes?	780 km
7	A metal cylinder is 10 cm in diameter and is 10 cm tall. Find its volume.	785 cm^3
8	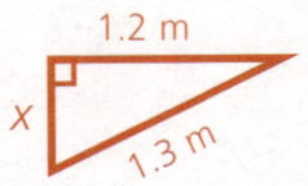 Write down the length of side x.	0.5 m
9	What is the order of rotational symmetry of a rectangle about its centre? 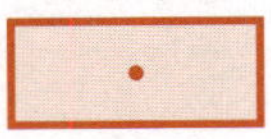	2
10	Eight bottles each have a capacity of 972 mℓ. Find their total capacity to the nearest litre.	8 ℓ

C

ANSWER

Mrs Bray sets off from Leeds to travel to Nottingham.
Mrs Jackson is travelling from Nottingham to Leeds.
They arrange to meet at the motorway service station.

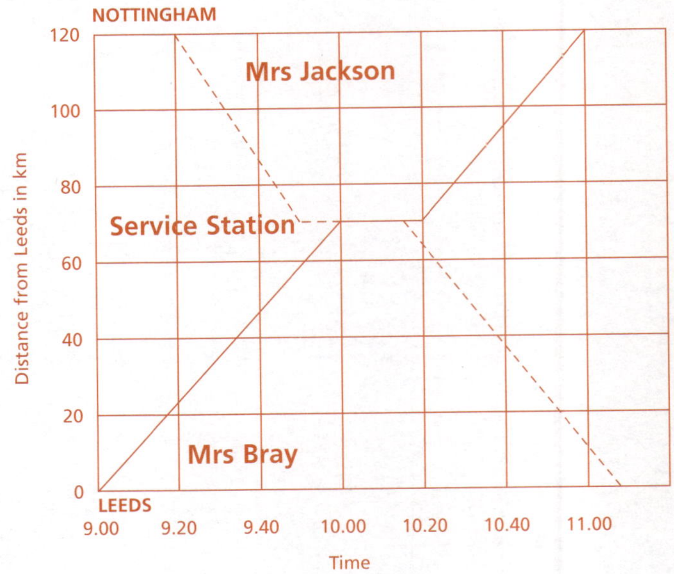

		ANSWER
1	At what time does Mrs Bray set off from Leeds?	9.00
2	At what time does Mrs Bray arrive at the service station?	10.00
3	How long does Mrs Bray take to reach the service station?	1 h
4	What is the distance in km from Leeds to the service station?	70 km
5	What is Mrs Bray's mean (average) speed in km/h between Leeds and the service station?	70 km/h
6	At what time does Mrs Jackson leave Nottingham?	9.20
7	How long does Mrs Jackson take to reach the service station?	0.5 h
8	What is Mrs Jackson's mean (average) speed in km/h between Nottingham and the service station?	100 km/h
9	How long does Mrs Bray stay at the service station?	20 min
10	How long does Mrs Jackson have to see Mrs Bray while they are both at the service station?	15 min
11	When Mrs Bray reaches Nottingham how far does Mrs Jackson have to travel to reach Leeds?	10 km
12	What is Mrs Bray's mean (average) speed in km/h for the whole journey from Leeds to Nottingham?	60 km/h

Section 2 Test 9

A — ANSWER

		ANSWER
1	$-17 + 25 =$	8
2	$(80 \times 5) \div (80 \div 5) =$	25
3	Add 2×10^3 and 3×10^2.	2300
4	Change $2\frac{4}{5}$ to a percentage.	280%
5	Add $\frac{3}{8}$ of 40 to $\frac{4}{5}$ of 80.	79
6	$1.2 \div 0.003 =$	400
7	$(3.5 - 3.3) \times (2.3 + 3.5) =$	1.16
8	Approximate 4.006 to 2 significant figures.	4.0
9	Give the answer to $2 \div 7$ correct to two significant figures.	0.29
10	If $p = 1$, $q = 2$, evaluate $\frac{pq}{p^2}$.	2
11	$\frac{2m + 4}{5} = 2$, so $m =$	3
12	Write in the next two terms of the sequence 1, 4, 9, 16, ___, ___	25, 36

B — ANSWER

1. If 8 articles cost £1 then 36 will cost — £ 4·50
2. How much is a 35% deposit on a £480 washing machine? — £ 168
3. $8\frac{1}{2}$ stones = — 119 lb
4. 3 gallons ÷ 6 = — 4 pints
5. Which three of the following were leap years? 1410, 1600, 1704, 1900, 1992 — 1600, 1704, 1992
6. How long does it take to travel 50 m at 45 km/h? — 4 s
7. An 8 cm square metal sheet has a 4 cm diameter circular hole cut into it. What area of metal remains? — 51.44 cm²
8. 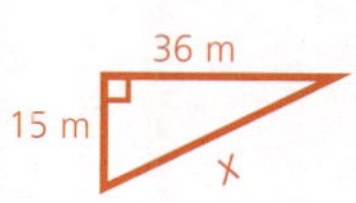

Write down the length of side x. — 39 m
9. What is the number of axes of symmetry of this letter H? 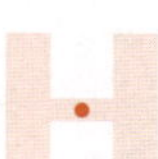 — 2
10. Find the approximate number of days in 5 months. — 150 days

C — ANSWER

Below is part of the timetable of trains from York to Manchester.
Notes: *a* is arrive, *d* is depart.

York	*d*	0625	0913	1115	1948	2148
Leeds	*d*	0703	1002	1202	2032	2233
Bradford	*a*	0723	1022	1222	2052	2253
Bradford	*d*	0726	1025	1225	2055	2256
Halifax	*d*	0737	1036	1236	2107	2308
Todmorden	*d*	0800	1059	1259	2129	2330
Rochdale	*d*	0814	1114	1314	2145	2346
Manchester	*a*	0839	1133	1333	2212	0009

1. How many of the trains leave York in the morning? — 3
2. How many of the trains arrive at Manchester between noon and midnight? — 2
3. How long do trains wait in Bradford? — 3 min
4. At what time does the 3-minutes-past-7 train from Leeds depart from Todmorden? — 0800
5. At what time does the 9.48 pm train from York leave Halifax? — 2308
6. At what time does the 5-to-9 train from Bradford depart from Rochdale? — 2145
7. What is the latest train from York that gets to Rochdale before 10.00 pm? — 1948
8. What is the latest train from Leeds that gets to Todmorden before 1.00 pm? — 1202
9. Which train from York travels the fastest to Leeds? — 0625
10. Between which two stations do trains travel for the shortest time? — Bradford to Halifax
11. How many minutes does it take for the last train from York to travel to Manchester? — 141 min
12. What is the shortest time in hours and minutes for the whole journey? — 2 h 14 min

Section 2 Test 10

A

		ANSWER
1	$-2 \times 5 =$	−10
2	$(80 + 5) \div (80 \div 5) =$	5 rem 5
3	Add 1.4×10^3 and 4.1×10^2.	1810
4	Express $1\frac{3}{4}$ as a ratio in its lowest terms.	7 : 4
5	Find the difference between 10% of 20 and 20% of 10?	0
6	$1.99 + 0.19 - 0.91 =$	1.27
7	$\frac{4.8 \times 0.6}{1.8} =$	1.6
8	Approximate 0.003325 to 1 significant figure.	0.003
9	Estimate to the nearest ten $\frac{555.3 + 444.8}{5.03 \times 3.99}$	50
10	If $h = 2$, $k = 3$, evaluate $\frac{5h}{3k}$ as a mixed number.	$1\frac{1}{9}$
11	$\frac{1}{a} = 2$, so $a =$	0.5
12	Write in the next two terms of the sequence 5 , 4 , 3 , 2 , 1 ,	0 , −1

B

		ANSWER
1	Find (a) the cost of 3 articles at £3·75 each and	(a) £ 11·25
	(b) the change from £20.	(b) £ 8·75
2	How much will 100 000 Greek drachma cost at 400 drachma to £1?	£ 250
3	33 ft 6 in =	11 yd 0 ft 6in
4	25 yd ÷ 10 =	2 yd 1 ft 6 in
5	How many hours in one week?	168 h
6	What is my speed if I travel $\frac{1}{3}$ mile in 2 minutes?	10 mph
7	A right angle triangle has sides of length 6 cm, 8 cm, 10 cm. Find its area.	24 cm²
8	 Write down the length of side x.	50 cm
9	What is the smallest angle through which the letter H can be turned so that it again looks like H? 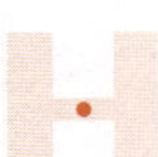	180°
10	Express 250 weeks to the nearest year.	5 yr

C

Natalie is checking the times of TV programmes.

BBC 1		ITV	
8.30 am	Breakfast Show	8.25 am	Disney Club
9.30 am	Kingdom Come	10.15 am	Story Keepers
10.15 am	See Hear	10.45 am	Morning Worship
10.45 am	Deutsch Plus	11.45 am	Mozambique Link
11.00 am	Chinese Art	12.00 pm	Country Churches
12.00 pm	Countryfile	12.30 pm	Newsweek
12.25 pm	Weather	12.55 pm	Regional News
12.30 pm	National News	1.00 pm	National News
12.40 pm	On the Record	1.10 pm	Politics
1.30 pm	EastEnders	2.00 pm	Murder, She Wrote
2.55 pm	Clothes Show	2.55 pm	Coronation Street
3.20 pm	Variety Awards	3.55 pm	Romance in Rome
4.00 pm	Football Match	5.35 pm	Princess Diana
6.10 pm	National News	6.30 pm	Calendar
6.25 pm	Weather	6.45 pm	National News
6.30 pm	Regional News	6.55 pm	Weather
6.35 pm	Red Nose Dish	7.00 pm	Bruce Forsyth
6.40 pm	Songs of Praise	7.30 pm	Coronation Street
7.15 pm	Antiques Show	8.00 pm	A Touch of Frost

		ANSWER
1	How many minutes does Disney Club last?	110 min
2	How many minutes of National News is there on BBC 1?	25 min
3	What is the total amount of Regional News on ITV?	5 min
4	How long is EastEnders on BBC1?	1 h 25 min
5	Which ITV programme begins at noon?	Country Churches
6	What time does the Football Match start in 24-hour clock time?	1600
7	How long is the longest programme on ITV?	1 h 50 min
8	Which programme is the longer, Princess Diana or the Variety Awards, and by how much?	Princess Diana 15 min

Natalie wants to record some programmes. She has a blank 180 minute tape and her video uses 24-hour clock times.

		ANSWER
9	What time should she set the video for the start of EastEnders?	1330
10	What time remains on the tape after recording EastEnders?	1 h 35 min
11	Is there enough time on the tape to record both EastEnders and Romance in Rome?	No
12	If Natalie records the early edition of Coronation Street straight after recording EastEnders will there be enough tape left to record the evening edition of Coronation Street as well?	Yes

Section 2 Test 11

A — ANSWER

1 $-35 \div 5 =$ **−7**

2 $(80 \div 5) - 80 =$ **−64**

3 Write in figures the fifth power of two. **32**

4 Change 4:5 to twentieths. **$\frac{16}{20}$**

5 Change $1\frac{2}{3}$ into (a) thirds (a) **$\frac{5}{3}$**

and (b) a ratio in its lowest terms. (b) **5 : 3**

6 $0.05 \div 0.5 =$ **0.1**

7 $\frac{32.4}{0.9 \times 0.2}$ **180**

8 Approximate 5.005 to 2 significant figures. **5.0**

9 Write (2.375×10^3) as a number correct to two significant figures. **2400**

10 If $a = 2$, $b = 3$, evaluate $a^2b + b^2a$. **30**

11 $\frac{24}{x + 7} = 2$, so $x =$ **5**

12 $(1.5)^2 =$ **2.25**

B — ANSWER

1 Find the cost of 100 articles at 8 for 50p. **£ 6·25**

2 I buy 25 books at £1·40 each and sell the lot for £28. How much do I lose? **£ 7**

3 200 in = **5 yd 1 ft 8 in**

4 $7\frac{1}{2}$ lb ÷ 12 = **10 oz**

5 How many minutes between 07.44 and 11.18? **214 min**

6 How long will it take a rocket moving at 12 km/s to travel 324 000 km? **7 h 30 min**

7 A stone slab is 3 ft long, 2 ft wide and 2 in thick. Find its volume in in³. **1728 in³**

8 Write down the height h of the triangle shown.

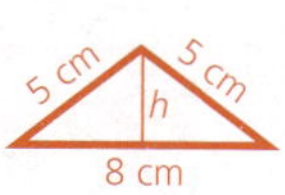

$h =$ **3 cm**

9 What is the order of rotational symmetry of the letter H about its centre?

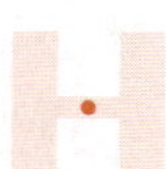

2

10 If 2000 identical boxes have a total mass of 1.88 t find the mass of a box to the nearest kg. **1 kg**

C — ANSWER

Tom has four number cards.

4 **6** **9** **1**

Each card has a single digit on it. Help Tom to arrange his cards to answer the following questions.

1 What is the smallest three-digit number Tom can make? **1 4 6**

2 What is the largest three-digit odd number Tom can make? **9 6 1**

3 What is the smallest four-digit number Tom can make? **1 4 6 9**

4 What is the largest four-digit even number Tom can make? **9 6 1 4**

5 What is the smallest two-digit square number Tom can make? **1 6**

6 What two-digit cubic number can Tom make? **6 4**

7 Which cards can Tom use to show 13²? **1 6 9**

8 Which cards can Tom use to show 31²? **9 6 1**

Tom arranges his cards in two pairs. The digits on each pair form a square number.

9 Which two square numbers did Tom make? **1 6 , 4 9**

Tom arranges his four cards to give the biggest number he can make and then rearranges them to give the smallest number.

10 What is the difference between these two numbers? **8172**

Tom takes two cards, adds the digits together, squares the result and writes down the answer. He finds he can then rearrange the two remaining cards to show this answer.

11 Which two digits did Tom add together? **1 , 6**

12 What answer did Tom get when he squared the result? **49**

Section 2 Test 12

A — ANSWER

1. $-2 \times -3 =$ — 6
2. $(80 \div 5) + (80 \times 5) =$ — 416
3. Fill in the blanks. $3^4 =$ 3 × 3 × 3 × 3 = 81
4. Write $\frac{5}{8}$ as a decimal correct to three places. — 0.625
5. Express $2\frac{3}{4}$ as a ratio in its lowest terms. — 11 : 4
6. $0.1 \times 0.2 \times 0.3 =$ — 0.006
7. $\left(\frac{12.8}{6.4}\right)^2 =$ — 4
8. Approximate 1 470 000 to 2 significant figures. — 1 500 000
9. Write (1.408×10^6) as a number correct to the nearest hundred thousand. — 1 400 000
10. If $x = 2$, $y = 3$, evaluate $x^3 - y$. — 5
11. $2x + 10 = 0$, so $x =$ — –5
12. $(0.6)^2 =$ — 0.36

B — ANSWER

1. Share £3·60 in the ratio 1:2. — £ 1·20 : £ 2·40
2. Which is the better buy (a) 25 for 40p or (b) 60 for £1? — (a)
3. 150 lb = — 10 st 10 lb
4. 2 ft $8\frac{1}{2}$ in × 6 = — 5 yd 1 ft 3 in
5. How many minutes between 21.53 and 02.42? — 289 min
6. What is my speed if I travel $\frac{1}{4}$ mile in $\frac{1}{2}$ minute? — 30 mph
7. A wooden beam is 10 ft long, 1 ft wide and 6 in thick. Find its volume in ft^3. — 5 ft^3
8. 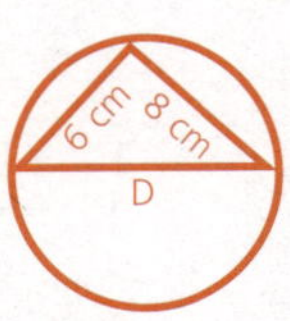

What size is the diameter D of the circle shown? D = — 10 cm
9. What is the order of rotational symmetry of a regular pentagon about its centre? 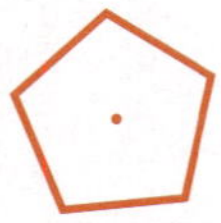 — 5
10. Five equal pieces of wood are cut from a plank 2.4 m long. What is the length of each piece of wood to the nearest 10 cm? — 50 cm

C — ANSWER

The children at Brightwell School are organising a Lucky Dip for the Summer Fair. Each prize has been carefully wrapped and placed in a large box. Visitors pay 20 pence a go and can choose one prize from the box. Since each prize is wrapped they will not know how lucky they have been until they unwrap their parcel.
The table shows how many of each prize have been put into the box.

Prize	Number
Choc Bar	30
Eraser	25
Balloon	50
Badge	10
Comb	10
Muesli Bar	20
Pen Set	5
TOTAL	150

Gareth is the first person to try the Lucky Dip.

1. How many balloons are in the box when Gareth has his first try? — 50
2. How many prizes are there in total when Gareth has his first try? — 150
3. Express as a fraction in its lowest terms the probability of Gareth choosing a balloon on his first try. — $\frac{1}{3}$
4. Express as a decimal the probability of Gareth choosing a choc bar on his first try. — 0.2
5. Express as a decimal the probability of Gareth NOT choosing a choc bar on his first try. — 0.8
6. What is the probability of Gareth choosing EITHER a choc bar OR a muesli bar on his first try? — 50 in 150
7. If Gareth chooses a choc bar on his first try what is the probability of choosing a muesli bar on his second try? — 20 in 149
8. If Gareth chooses a choc bar on his first try what is the probability of choosing another choc bar on his second try? — 29 in 149

When Lucy tries the Lucky Dip exactly half of the prizes have gone but noone has won a pen set.

9. What is the probability of Lucy choosing a pen set on her first try? — $\frac{5}{75}$
10. How many tries would Lucy have to have to be CERTAIN of winning a pen set? — 71
11. How much would this number of tries cost her? — £ 14·20
12. Is it possible that Lucy COULD win a pen set with LESS tries than this? — Yes
Explain your answer. She could win with any of her first 70 tries.

Section 2 Revision Test

		ANSWER
1	What is half of −16?	−8
2	$(72 - 48) \times \frac{72}{48} =$	36
3	$(3.25 \times 10^3) + (3.25 \times 10^2) =$	3575
4	$56\% > \frac{5}{6}$. TRUE or FALSE?	FALSE
5	Add $\frac{2}{3}$ of 30 to $\frac{3}{4}$ of 40.	50
6	$5 \div 0.5 =$	10
7	$54 \div (5.4 - 4.5) =$	60
8	Approximate 0.0789 to 1 significant figure.	0.08
9	Calculate $401 \div 5$ correct to 2 significant figures.	80
10	If $a = 2$, $b = 3$, $c = 4$, $d = 5$, find the value of $\frac{bc}{a} + d$.	11
11	$\frac{1}{4}(x + 5) = 2$, so $x =$	3
12	What is the smallest number that is exactly divisible by 2, 3 and 5 ?	30
13	If six pens cost £2·20, then 15 pens cost	£ 5·50
14	I put down a 30% deposit on a carpet costing £420. How much is left to pay?	£ 294
15	Change 2 yd 1 ft 5 in to inches.	89 in
16	Reduce 10 stone by 10%. Give your answer in lb.	126 lb
17	What date is the 100th day of a leap year?	9th of April
18	A powder has a density of 1800 kg/m^3. What is the volume of 450 kg of the powder?	0.25 m^3
19	A cylindrical tank is 1.2 m tall and has a volume of 3 m^3. What is the area of the base of the tank?	2.5 m^2
20	A square has sides of length 5 cm. What is the length of the diagonal to the nearest cm?	7 cm
21	What is the order of rotational symmetry of a rectangle about its centre?	2
22	16 bottles each have a capacity of 492 mℓ. Find their total capacity to the nearest litre.	8 litres
23	A point P has coordinates (5, 3). What are the coordinates of the reflection of P in the *y*-axis?	(−5 , 3)
24	An architect draws a plan of a school to a scale of 1:500. If the school is 45 m long what is its length on the plan?	9 cm
25	Using the digits 2, 3, 5, 8 subtract the largest two-digit even number from the smallest three digit even number. Each digit can be used only once in each number.	156

Section 2 Revision Test

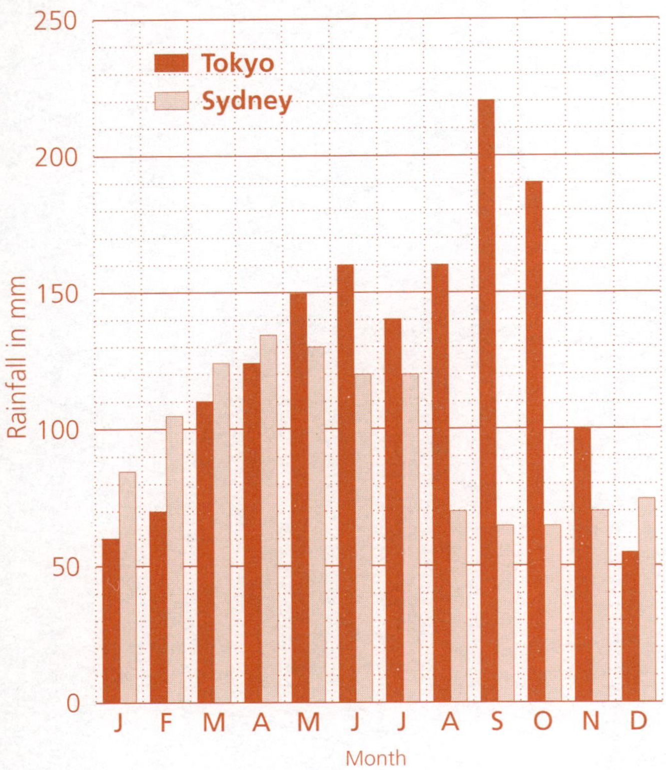

Graph of total monthly rainfall for Tokyo, Japan and Sydney, Australia

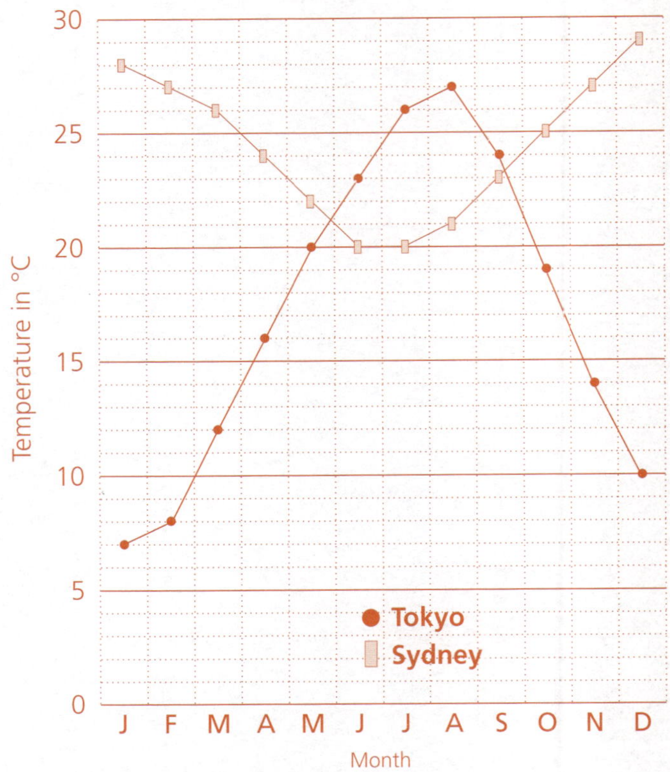

Graph of maximum monthly temperature for Tokyo, Japan and Sydney, Australia

Look carefully at the graphs above and answer the following questions.

		ANSWER
26	Which is the wettest month in Sydney?	April
27	Which month shows the greatest difference between the rainfall in Tokyo and the rainfall in Sydney?	September
28	In which month is the rainfall in Tokyo and Sydney most nearly the same?	April
29	How much rain falls in Tokyo during its driest month?	55 mm
30	What is the RANGE of rainfall in Sydney?	70 mm
31	Which is the hottest month in Sydney?	December
32	Which is the coldest month in Tokyo?	January
33	Which month shows the greatest difference between the temperature in Tokyo and the temperature in Sydney?	January
34	In which month is the maximum temperature in Tokyo and Sydney most nearly the same?	September
35	What is the RANGE of maximum temperature in Sydney?	9°C
36	What is the temperature in Tokyo during its wettest month?	24°C
37	Between which two months in Sydney is there no change in both rainfall and temperature?	June , July
38	What is the mean maximum temperature in Tokyo during its hottest four-month period?	25°C
39	What is the total rainfall in Sydney during its four hottest months?	335 mm
40	What is the total rainfall in Tokyo during its three coldest months?	185 mm

Mental Arithmetic 6

Name of student		Diagnostic Chart for Section 3 Indicate where the student has difficulty											
		1	2	3	4	5	6	7	8	9	10	11	12
Test 1	Part A												
	Part B												
	Part C												
Test 2	Part A												
	Part B												
	Part C												
Test 3	Part A												
	Part B												
	Part C												
Test 4	Part A												
	Part B												
	Part C												
Test 5	Part A												
	Part B												
	Part C												
Test 6	Part A												
	Part B												
	Part C												
Test 7	Part A												
	Part B												
	Part C												
Test 8	Part A												
	Part B												
	Part C												
Test 9	Part A												
	Part B												
	Part C												
Test 10	Part A												
	Part B												
	Part C												
Test 11	Part A												
	Part B												
	Part C												
Test 12	Part A												
	Part B												
	Part C												

Section 3 Test 1

A

		ANSWER
1	What is the remainder when 323 is divided by 7?	rem 1
2	(930 + 470) ÷ 14 =	100
3	Write in figures eighty-nine hundred.	8900
4	Express $\frac{1}{8}$ as a decimal.	0.125
5	$3\frac{3}{4} \times 40 =$	150
6	2.8 – 0.07 =	2.73
7	0.5 × (2.5 + 7.2) =	4.85
8	Round 5.0827496 to the nearest thousandth.	5.083
9	Calculate correct to two significant figures 12.084 ÷ 6	2.0
10	If $a = 4$, $b = 5$ and $c = 6$ find the value of $a^2 + b^2 + c^2$.	77
11	$5u + 11 = 46$, so $u =$	7
12	Write in the next two terms of the sequence 100 , 10 , 1 , 0.1 ,	0.01 , 0.001

B

		ANSWER
1	I buy 16 articles at £2·75 each. How much change from £50?	£ 6
2	The price of a £9800 car rises by 6%.What is the new cost?	£ 10 388
3	75 mm is approximately	3 in
4	1 m^2 =	10 000 cm^2
5	How many days inclusive from 15.10.1997 to 5.2.1998?	114 days
6	Melanie runs 200 m in 24 s. What is her speed in km/h?	30 km/h
7	A circular concrete stepping stone is 40 cm in diameter and 5 cm thick. Find its volume.	6280 cm^3

8 

If O is the centre of the circle, write down the size of angle x. x = 60°

9 What is the number of axes of symmetry of this shape?  4

10 Find the cost of six books at £4·95 each to the nearest £1. £ 30

C

ANSWER

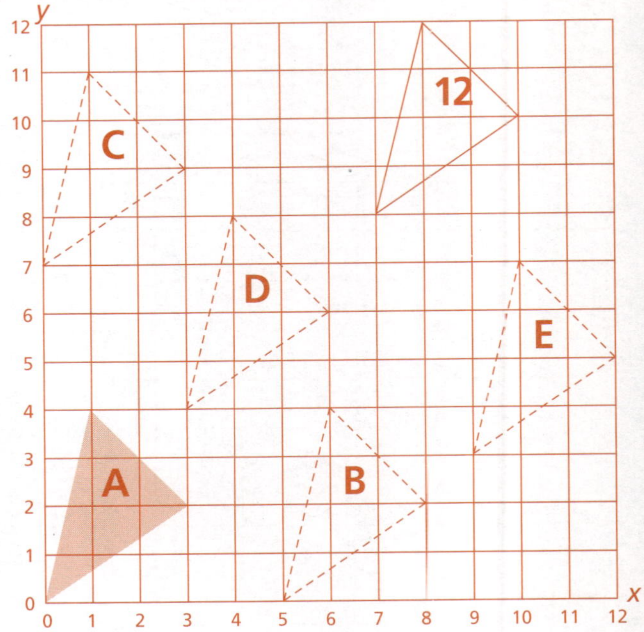

1	Write down the corner coordinates of triangle A.	(0 , 0) (3 , 2) (1 , 4)
2	Triangle A is translated to position B. Write down the corner coordinates of the triangle when in position B.	(5 , 0) (8 , 2) (6 , 4)
3	What happens to the x-values of the coordinates of the triangle when it is translated to position B?	increased by 5
4	What happens to the y-values of the coordinates of the triangle when it is translated to position B?	stay the same
5	Use your answers to questions 3 and 4 to complete the statement: The mapping $(x,y) \rightarrow (x + \underline{5}, y)$ translates triangle A to position B.	
6	Write down the corner coordinates of the triangle when translated to position C.	(0 , 7) (3 , 9) (1 , 11)
7	Use your answer to question 6 to complete the statement: The mapping $(x,y) \rightarrow (x, y + \underline{7})$ translates triangle A to position C.	
8	Write down the corner coordinates of the triangle when translated to position D.	(3 , 4) (6 , 6) (4 , 8)
9	Complete the statement: The mapping $(x, y) \rightarrow (x + \underline{3}, y + \underline{4})$ translates triangle A to position D.	
10	Complete the statement: The mapping $(x, y) \rightarrow (x + \underline{9}, y + \underline{3})$ translates triangle A to position E.	
11	Triangle A is translated by the mapping $(x, y) \rightarrow (x + 7, y + 8)$. Write down the values of the corner coordinates when the triangle is translated by this mapping to its new position.	(7 , 8) (10 , 10) (8 , 12)
12	On the grid above sketch in the new position of the triangle.	

Section 3 Test 2

A

		ANSWER
1	Write down the product of 142 and 9.	1278
2	(72 + 56) ÷ (72 – 56) =	8
3	Write in figures nineteen hundred and eight.	1908
4	Arrange in ascending order $\frac{3}{4}$, $\frac{2}{3}$, $\frac{4}{5}$, $\frac{5}{8}$, $\frac{1}{2}$	$\frac{1}{2} < \frac{5}{8} < \frac{2}{3} < \frac{3}{4} < \frac{4}{5}$
5	Divide 70 in the ratio 2:5.	20 : 50
6	0.705 + 0.09 + 1.03 =	1.825
7	0.4 × (4 – 0.08) =	1.568
8	Round 16.2534865 to the nearest ten thousandth.	16.2535
9	Calculate correct to three decimal places 2.43 ÷ 9	0.270
10	If $x = 2$, $y = 3$, $z = 5$, find the value of $x^2 + y^2 + z^2$.	38
11	$3p^2 = 48$, so p =	4
12	Express 42 as a product of three prime numbers.	2 × 3 × 7 = 42

B

		ANSWER
1	Share £15 in the ratio 3:2.	£ 9 : £ 6
2	I buy a box of 48 oranges for £5 and sell them at 15p each. What is my profit?	£ 2·20
3	10 cm is approximately	4 in
4	1 ha =	10 000 m²
5	Which of these years was in the 2nd millennium BC? 2850 BC, 1725 BC, 986 BC?	1725 BC
6	How long will it take to travel 1500 m at 90 km/h?	1 min
7	A wooden disk 20 cm in diameter has a circular hole 10 cm in diameter cut into it. What area remains?	235.5 cm²
8	At what angle do the diagonals of a kite cross each other?	90°
9	What is the order of rotational symmetry of this shape about its centre? 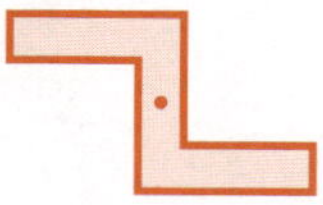	2
10	Approximate 3098 mm to the nearest cm.	310 cm

C

ANSWER

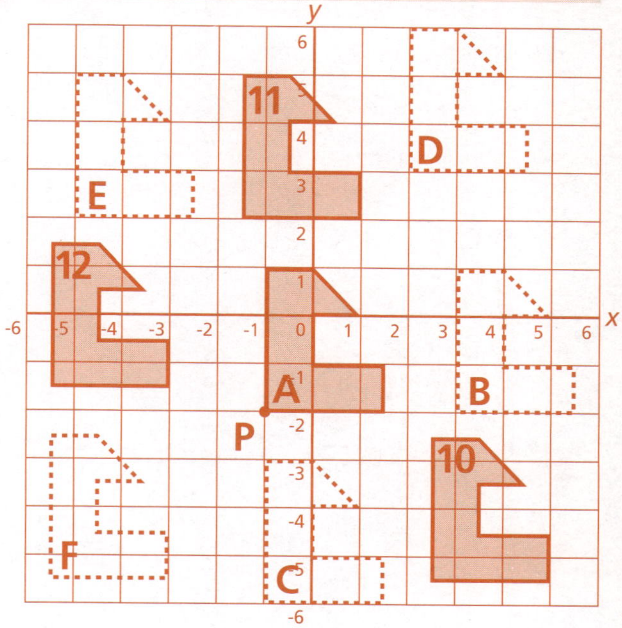

		ANSWER
1	Write down the coordinates of point P on shape A.	(–1 , –2)
2	Write down the mapping which translates shape A to position B. (x,y) ⟶	(x + 4 , y)
3	Write down the mapping which translates shape A to position C. (x,y) ⟶	(x , y – 4)
4	Write down the mapping which translates shape A to position D. (x,y) ⟶	(x + 3 , y + 5)
5	Write down the mapping which translates shape A to position E. (x,y) ⟶	(x – 4 , y + 4)
6	Write down the mapping which translates shape A to position F. (x,y) ⟶	(x – 4.5 , y – 3.5)
7	Write down the horizontal mapping that will bring point P to the y-axis. (x,y) ⟶	(x + 1 , y)
8	Write down the vertical mapping that will bring point P to the x-axis. (x,y) ⟶	(x , y + 2)
9	Write down the mapping that will bring point P to the origin. (x,y) ⟶	(x + 1 , y + 2)
10	On the above grid draw in the position of shape A when translated by the mapping (x,y) ⟶ (x + 3.5 , y – 3.5)	
11	On the above grid draw in the position of shape A when translated by the mapping (x,y) ⟶ (x – 0.5, y + 4.5)	
12	On the above grid draw in the position of shape A when translated by the mapping (x,y) ⟶ (x – 4.5, y +0.5)	

Section 3 Test 3

A — ANSWER

1 Write down the sum of 526 and 625. **1151**

2 $((15 + 45) \div 3) \div 2 =$ **10**

3 Write in figures forty six thousand and forty six. **46 046**

4 $33\% > \frac{1}{3}$. TRUE or FALSE? **FALSE**

5 Reduce 120 by $33\frac{1}{3}\%$. **80**

6 $2.2 \times 0.03 =$ **0.066**

7 $\frac{8.4}{0.3 + 0.4} =$ **12**

8 Round 0.00985 to the nearest thousandth. **0.010**

9 Estimate to the nearest ten $\frac{48.97 \times 52.6}{25.12}$. **100**

10 If $m = 4$, $n = 5$, $q = 6$ find the value of $m(q^2 - n^2)$. **44**

11 $\sqrt{r} = 9$, so $r =$ **81**

12 Write down the prime factors of 20. **2** × **2** × **5** = 20

B — ANSWER

1 If 45 envelopes cost £1·35 how much is this per envelope? **3p**

2 Calculate the interest at 7.5% on a loan of £4000. £ **300**

3 60 cm is approximately **2 ft**

4 $1 \text{ km}^2 =$ **$1\,000\,000 \text{ m}^2$**

5 In a race Mary beat the previous school record of 23.17 s by $\frac{31}{100}$ s. What was Mary's new time? **22.86 s**

6 How long will it take to travel 42 km at 18 km/h? **2 h 20 min**

7 A tank of volume 9 m^3 has a square base of side 1.5 m. How tall is the tank? **4 m**

8 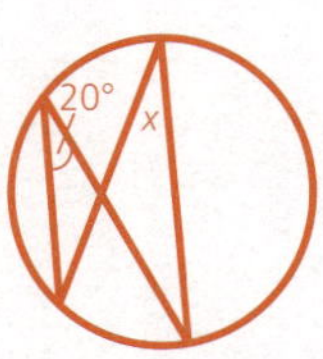

Write down the size of angle x. $x =$ **20 °**

9 

What is the number of axes of symmetry of this shape? **1**

10 Approximate 355 in to the nearest yard. **10 yd**

C — ANSWER

The table shows a spreadsheet that Karen used to investigate the angle properties of regular polygons. Two cells are empty. The diagram of a hexagon shows how Karen labelled the centre and interior angles.

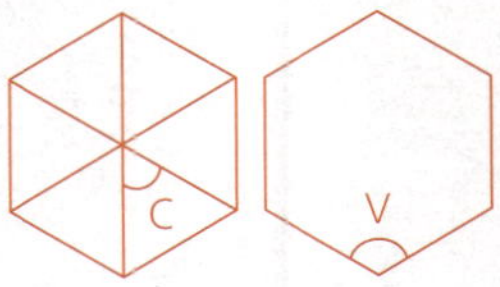

	A	B	C	D
1	Number of sides, N	Centre angle, C	Interior angle, V	Sum of interior angles
2	3	120	60	180
3	4	90	90	360
4	5	72	108	540
5	6	60	120	720
6	7	51.4	128.6	900
7	8	45	135	1080
8	9	40	140	1260
9	10	36	144	1440

1 Which row of the spreadsheet represents a hexagon? **5**

2 What shape is represented by row 3 of the spreadsheet? **square**

3 The formula used in the spreadsheet to calculate the angle at the centre of a hexagon was 360 ÷ A5. What value does this give for the centre angle? **60**

4 Into which empty cell should this value be entered? **B5**

5 What formula was used to find the centre angle of a ten-sided decagon? **360 ÷ A9**

6 To find the interior angle of a pentagon the formula 180 – B4 was used. What value of angle does this give? **108**

7 Into which empty cell should this value be entered? **C4**

8 What formula was used in the spreadsheet to find the interior angle of a seven-sided heptagon? **180 – B6**

9 What value results from using the formula C9*A9? **1440**

10 Which cell contains this value? **D9**

11 What does this value represent? **sum of interior angles of decagon**

12 What formula was used to find the sum of the interior angles of an octagon? **C7*A7**

Section 3 Test 4

A — ANSWER

1 Write down the difference between 308 and 803. ______ 495

2 $45 \div ((3 \times 3) + (2 \times 3)) =$ ______ 3

3 Write two thousand and seventy eight in standard notation. ______ 2.078×10^3

4 Arrange in descending order. 0.81, $\frac{8}{10}$, 1.08, 0.18

1.08 > 0.81 > $\frac{8}{10}$ > 0.18

5 Divide 160 in the ratio 3:5. ______ 60 : 100

6 $4.8 \div 8 =$ ______ 0.6

7 $\frac{8.4}{0.3 \times 0.4} =$ ______ 70

8 Write 1.503 correct to three significant figures. ______ 1.50

9 $5 < \frac{14 \times 21}{42} < 10$ TRUE or FALSE? ______ TRUE

10 If $a = 5$, $b = 3$, find the value of $b^3 - a^2$. ______ 2

11 $\frac{1}{2}x^2 = 12.5$, so $x =$ ______ 5

12 Write in the next two terms of the sequence.

$1, \frac{1}{2}, \frac{1}{4}, \frac{1}{8}$, $\frac{1}{16}$, $\frac{1}{32}$

B — ANSWER

1 If 500 sheets of card cost £12·50 how many sheets do I get for £1? ______ 40

2 I exchange £220 into Spanish pesetas at 200 pesetas to £1. How many pesetas do I get? ______ 44 000 pesetas

3 90 cm is approximately ______ 1 yd

4 $1 \text{ m}^3 =$ ______ $1\ 000\ 000 \text{ cm}^3$

5 Change 18 minutes to midnight to 24-hour clock notation. ______ 23.42

6 Joanne runs 180 m in 24 seconds. What is her speed in km/h? ______ 27 km/h

7 A cylindrical tank 2 m tall has a volume of 6.28 m^3. What is the tank's diameter? ______ 2 m

8 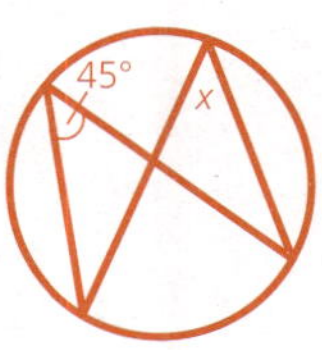

Write down the size of angle x. $x =$ ______ 45°

9 

What is the order of rotational symmetry of this shape about its centre? ______ 1

10 Five boxes have a mass of 2925 g each. Find the total mass to the nearest kg. ______ 15 kg

C — ANSWER

Class Six have some films they want to develop and print. They decide to send them to PrestoPrint. The mail order price list is shown below.

PRESTOPRINT – DEVELOPING AND PRINTING – MAIL ORDER PRICE LIST							
Developing and printing	Exp.	No. of films sent	First set of prints	Cost of first sets	Extra set of prints	Cost of extra sets	Total cost
6″ × 4″	24		£2·55	£	£1·44	£	£
6″ × 4″	36	3	£3·55	£10·65	£1·94	£	£10·65
7″ × 5″	24	2	£3·99	£7·98	£2·50	£5·00	£12·98
7″ × 5″	36	1	£4·99	£4·99	£3·00	£	£4·99
8.5″ × 6″	24	2	£5·95	£11·90	£4·00	£8·00	£19·90
8.5″ × 6″	36		£6·95	£	£5·00	£	£
TOTAL COST OF PRINTING AND DEVELOPING							£48·52
TOTAL NUMBER OF FILMS		8	POSTAGE AT 95p PER FILM				£7·60
TOTAL COST OF ORDER INCLUDING POSTAGE							£56·12

Jim has already put his order on the list.

1 How many films is Jim sending to PrestoPrint? ______ 2

2 Are Jim's films 24-exposure films or 36-exposure films? ______ 24

3 What size prints is Jim sending for? ______ 7″ x 5″

4 Why is the cost of Jim's first set of prints £7·98 and not £3·99? ______ he has sent 2 films

5 What will it cost Jim for the extra set of prints from both the films he sends? £ ______ 5·00

6 What is the total cost of Jim's order? £ ______ 12·98

Zoe has three 36-exposure films to send. She wants 6″x 4″ prints but she does not want any extra prints. Write Zoe's order on the form above.

7 What will it cost Zoe for her first set of prints? £ ______ 10·65

8 What is the total cost of Zoe's order (without postage)? £ ______ 10·65

Brian has two 24-exposure films and one 36-exposure film to send. He wants 8.5″ x 6″ prints and an extra set from the 24-exposure films and 7″ x 5″ prints but no extra set from the 36-exposure film. Write Brian's order on the form above.

9 What is the total cost of Brian's order (without postage)? £ ______ 24·89

10 What is the total cost of printing and developing all the films? £ ______ 48·52

11 What is the postage at 95p per film for the total number of films that Jim, Zoe and Brian are sending to PrestoPrint? £ ______ 7·60

12 What is the total cost of the order including postage? £ ______ 56·12

Fill in the form to show the complete order and the total cost.

Section 3 Test 5

A

		ANSWER
1	Write down the remainder when 85 is divided by 9.	rem 4
2	$(45 \div (3 \times 3)) + (2 \times 3) =$	11
3	Express 27 as a power of 3.	3^3
4	Express the ratio 6:25 as a decimal.	0.24
5	Add 20% of 30 to 40% of 50.	26
6	$8 \div 0.25 =$	32
7	$(0.5 \times 0.2) + (0.5 \div 0.2) =$	2.6
8	Round 9.997 (a) to 2 decimal places	(a) 10.00
	(b) to 2 significant figures.	(b) 10
9	$5 < \dfrac{3602}{61 \times 9} < 10$. TRUE or FALSE?	TRUE
10	If $h = 2$, $k = 3$, find the value of $hk^2 + h^2k$.	30
11	$2k - 5 = k$, so $k =$	5
12	List those numbers (except 1) that are factors of BOTH 18 and 30.	2, 3, 6

B

		ANSWER
1	I buy 3 cinema tickets for £2·80 each. How much change do I get from £10?	£ 1·60
2	A £150 bicycle is reduced by 12% in a sale. Find the new price.	£ 132
3	80 inches is approximately	2 m
4	1 g =	1000 mg
5	How many minutes in one day?	1440 min
6	How long will it take to travel 84 km at 48 km/h?	1 h 45 min
7	A tablet is 10 mm in diameter and 4 mm thick. Find the volume of 100 tablets.	31 400 mm^3
8	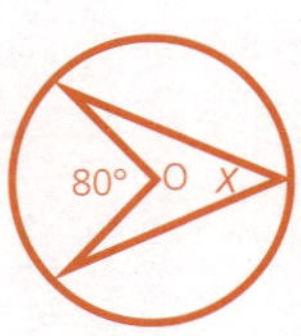 If O is the centre of the circle, what size is angle x?	$x =$ 40°
9	 What is the number of axes of symmetry of this road sign?	0
10	Approximate 12 lb 13 oz to the nearest stone.	1 stone

C

The diagram shows a plan of Mountjoy Park.
The grid lines are spaced 1 cm apart.

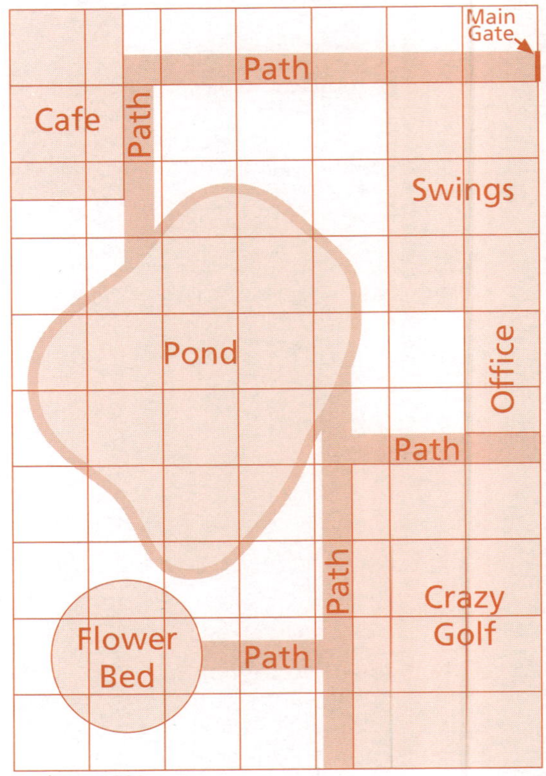

Scale 1 : 1000

		ANSWER
1	What distance in metres is represented by 1 cm on the plan?	10 m
2	Estimate the area used for the swings.	600 m^2
3	Estimate the area used for crazy golf.	1000 m^2
4	Estimate the area of the office.	160 m^2
5	Estimate the area of the pond to nearest 100 m^2. (Hint: count part squares equal to half or more as full squares and ignore squares less than half).	1300 m^2
6	If the pond has a mean depth of 60 cm estimate the volume of water to the nearest 100 m^3.	800 m^3
7	Estimate of the nearest 10 m the length of the path around the pond.	130 m
8	Estimate the diameter of the flower bed.	20 m
9	Estimate the area of the flower bed to the nearest 100 m^2.	300 m^2
10	Estimate the width of the straight paths. (Hint: look carefully at the paths near the cafe and the crazy golf).	4 m
11	Estimate to the nearest 10 m the total length of the straight paths.	160 m
12	Estimate to the nearest 10 m the distance along paths by the shortest route from the main gate to the flower bed.	170 m

Section 3 Test 6

A

ANSWER

1 Multiply the sum of 36 and 25 by their difference. 671

2 $(45 \div (2 + 3)) \times (3 + 3) =$ 54

3 Express 128 as a power of 2. 2^7

4 Express $1\frac{1}{2}$ as a ratio in its lowest terms. 3 : 2

5 Divide 33 in the ratio 8:3. 24 : 9

6 $0.7 - 7 =$ −6.3

7 $\dfrac{6.5}{0.6 + 0.7} =$ 5

8 Round 0.0909 to
(a) 3 decimal places 0.091

(b) 3 significant figures. 0.0909

9 Estimate to the nearest thousand
$\dfrac{(4.01 \times 10^3) \times (2.98 \times 10^3)}{1.99 \times 10^3}$ 6000

10 If $p = 4$, $r = 3$
find the value of $\dfrac{p^2 + 8}{2r}$. 4

11 $\dfrac{4}{n} = 2$, so $n =$ 2

12 What is the largest number that divides exactly into BOTH 45 and 72? 9

B

ANSWER

1 I buy a season ticket for £80 and make 32 journeys. How much per journey? £ 2·50

2 I buy a £182 refrigerator with 52 equal instalments. How much is each payment? £ 3·50

3 $4\frac{1}{2}$ lb is approximately 2 kg

4 65 kg × 20 = 1 t 300 kg

5 Write in 24-hour clock notation seven minutes past midnight. 00.07

6 When a ball is thrown it travels 1 m in 0.05 s. What is its speed in km/h? 72 km/h

7 How many tiles 20 cm square are needed to cover a floor measuring 4 m x 3 m? 300

8 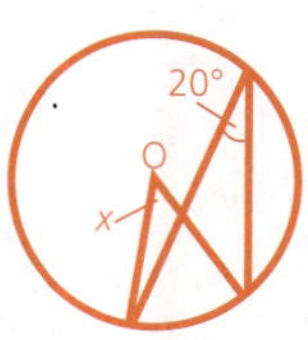

If O is the centre of the circle what size is angle x? $x =$ 40°

9 
What is the number of axes of symmetry of this shape? 2

10 Find the area of a carpet measuring 290 cm long and 88 cm wide to the nearest m². 3 m²

C

ANSWER

The map shows some of the main roads in Cumbria and the Lake District. The grid lines are spaced 1 cm apart.

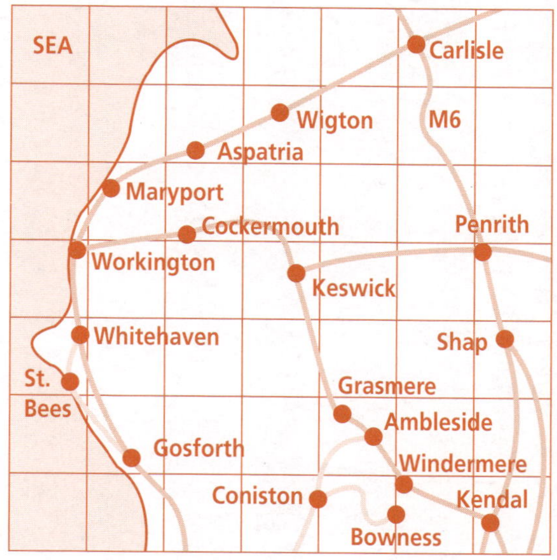

Scale 1 : 1 000 000

1 What distance in km is represented by 1 cm on the map? 10 km

2 The distance from Gosforth to Carlisle "as-the-crow-flies" (i.e. in a straight line) is 65 km. How far apart are these two towns on the map? 6.5 cm

Estimate to the nearest 10 km the distances along the following routes. You may use a ruler to help you.

3 Carlisle to the seaside town of Maryport 40 km

4 Penrith to St. Bees via Cockermouth 70 km

5 Coniston to Carlisle by the shortest route 90 km

6 Kendal to Aspatria "as-the-crow-flies" 60 km

7 What area (in km²) is represented by 1 cm² on the map? 100 km²

8 What area is represented by the whole map? 4900 km²

9 By counting squares estimate what area of sea is shown by the map? 1000 km²

10 What percentage (to nearest 10%) of the whole map shows sea? 20%

11 If the map above were redrawn to a scale of 1 : 100 000 would it be larger or smaller than the one shown? larger

12 If the map were redrawn to a scale of 1 : 50 000 what would be the straight line distance in cm from Gosforth to Carlisle on the map? 130 cm

Section 3 Test 7

A — ANSWER

1 Write down the sum of the squares of 5 and 6. — 61

2 $((2 + 3) \times 5) + 5 =$ — 30

3 Write $2^2 \times 2^3$ as (a) a number — (a) 32
(b) a power of two. — (b) 2^5

4 Express 450% as
(a) a fraction in its lowest terms — (a) $\frac{9}{2}$
(b) a ratio in its lowest terms. — (b) 9 : 2

5 $3 \div \frac{1}{4} =$ — 12

6 $3.5 \times 0.3 =$ — 1.05

7 $\frac{2.4 \times 1.8}{2.4 - 1.8} =$ — 7.2

8 Round 0.011 to
(a) one decimal place — (a) 0.0
(b) one significant figure. — (b) 0.01

9 Estimate to the nearest hundred $\frac{(3 \times 10^3) \times (5 \times 10^3)}{10^4}$ — 1500

10 If $u = 4$, $v = 5$, $w = 6$ find the value of $3v^2 - (2u^2 + w^2)$ — 7

11 $\frac{3}{p} - \frac{1}{2} = \frac{1}{4}$, so $p =$ — 4

12 Write down the highest common factor of 30 and 48. — 6

B — ANSWER

1 Share £450 in the ratio 4:5. — £ 200 : £ 250

2 Shirts at £9·50 each are reduced by 10%. How much do I save if I buy 3 shirts? — £ 2·85

3 9 litres is approximately — 2 gallons

4 18.4 kg ÷ 8 = 2 kg 300 g
= 2.3 kg

5 At 8.25 am a cooker is set to switch on $5\frac{1}{2}$ hours later. At what time does it come on? — 1.55 pm

6 How long will it take a snail to move 1 m at 5 mm/s? — 3 min 20 s

7 How many packets measuring 6 cm × 8 cm × 15 cm can be fitted into a box measuring 24 cm × 30 cm × 60 cm? — 60

8 A parallelogram is drawn so that its smallest angle is half the size of its largest angle. What size is each angle? — 60° , 120°

9 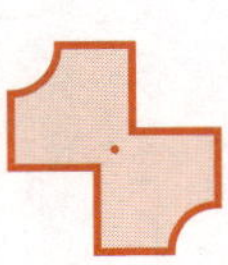
What is the order of rotational symmetry of this shape about its centre? — 2

10 A tank of water is 310 cm long, 195 cm wide, and is 95 cm deep. Find its approximate volume to the nearest cubic metre. — 6 m^3

C — ANSWER

The pie chart shows the results of a survey in a large city into how people travel to work.

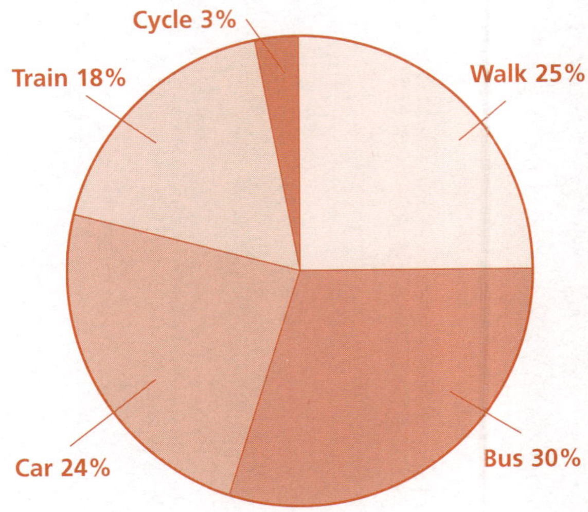

A factory in the city has 513 workers. Use the pie chart to estimate the approximate number of factory workers who travel to work by different means. (Hint: round the number of factory workers to the nearest 100 before you start.)

1 Travel to work by bus — 150

2 Walk to work — 125

3 Go to work by train — 90

4 Cycle to work — 15

5 Do NOT use a car to go to work — 380

An office block in the city has 4897 workers. Round this figure to a suitable value to help you to estimate the approximate number of office workers who:

6 Go to work by bus — 1500

7 Either walk or cycle to work — 1400

8 Do NOT use a train to get to work — 4100

9 Do NOT use a car to get to work — 3800

In this city about one million people go to work each day. Use this figure and the information in the pie chart to help you to answer the following questions:

10 A train holds about 500 people. Approximately how many trains will be needed for those who go to work by train? — 360

11 About one half of all the people who go to work by car are passengers. Approximately how many people who go to work each day by car are passengers? — 120 000

12 About two-thirds of bus passengers are women. What is the approximate number of women who travel to work by bus? — 200 000

Section 3 Test 8

A

		ANSWER
1	Write down the difference between the squares of 6 and 7.	13
2	$\frac{35 \times 45}{5 \times 5} =$	63
3	Write $2^{(2+3)}$ as (a) a power of two	(a) 2^5
	(b) a number.	(b) 32
4	Complete the blanks to make these fractions equivalent.	$\frac{3}{5} = \frac{6}{10} = \frac{12}{20} = \frac{60}{100}$
5	$\frac{3}{10} + \frac{3}{5} =$	$\frac{9}{10}$
6	$2 - 0.2 - 0.22 =$	1.58
7	$\frac{1}{0.5} - 0.5 =$	1.5
8	14.098 becomes 14.10 when rounded to how many decimal places?	2
9	$0.1 < \frac{0.6}{0.5} < 1.0$ TRUE or FALSE ?	FALSE
10	If $u = 4$, $v = 5$, $w = 6$ find the value of $3v^2 - (2u^2 - w^2)$.	79
11	$\frac{24}{3(x+5)} = 1$, so $x =$	3
12	Write down the smallest multiple of BOTH 6 and 9.	18

B

		ANSWER
1	If 50 stamps cost £10·50 how much for 20 stamps?	£ 4·20
2	How many Dutch guilders at 2.65 guilders to £1 can I buy for £300?	795 guilders
3	1 litre is approximately	2 pints
4	80 m ÷ 25 =	3.2 m = 3 m 20 cm
5	Karina works three shifts of $7\frac{1}{4}$ hours, $7\frac{1}{2}$ hours and $5\frac{1}{2}$ hours. How many hours altogether?	20 h 15 min
6	A car travels at 30 mph. How far will it go in 1 second? [1 mile = 1760 yd]	44 ft
7	A roll of tape is 25 mm wide and 50 m long. What is its area in m^2?	1.25 m^2
8	The acute angle of a rhombus is 40°. How big is the obtuse angle?	140°
9	 What is the number of axes of symmetry of this shape?	1
10	40 cartons each have a capacity of 248 mℓ. Find the total capacity to the nearest litre.	10 ℓ

C

ANSWER

Amy is investigating the area of rectangles. She calculates the areas by multiplying the length by the breadth and plots graphs of the results. Graph B represents rectangles of area 240 cm^2.

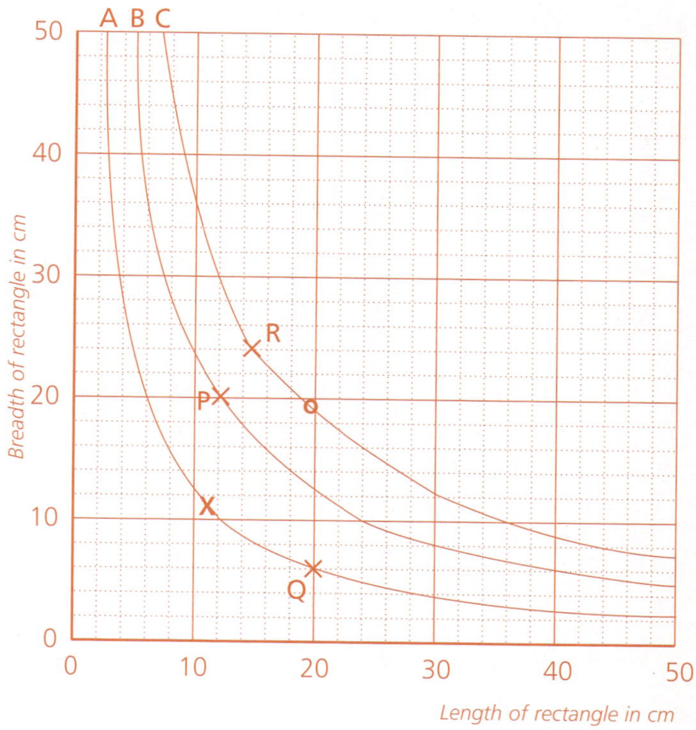

		ANSWER
1	What length of rectangle is represented by point P?	12 cm
2	What breadth of rectangle is represented by point P?	20 cm
3	What area of rectangle is represented by point P?	240 cm^2
4	What length of rectangle is represented by point Q?	20 cm
5	What breadth of rectangle is represented by point Q?	6 cm
6	What area of rectangle is represented by point Q?	120 cm^2
7	What area of rectangle is represented by all points that lie on graph A?	120 cm^2
8	Mark with an x the point on graph A that represents a square.	
9	Use the graph to help you to estimate the length of the side of this square.	11 cm
10	What area of rectangle is represented by point R?	360 cm^2
11	Mark with an o the point that represents a square of area 360 cm^2.	
12	Use the graph to help you to estimate the length of the sides of this square.	19 cm

Section 3 Test 9

A

ANSWER

1 Add the square of 2 to its cube. 12

2 $\frac{32 \times 72}{8 \times 12} =$ 24

3 Write $2^5 \div 2^2$ as (a) a number (a) 8

(b) a power of two. (b) 2^3

4 Which two of the following are equal? $\frac{3}{8}$, 3.8, 3:8, 38%, $3\frac{1}{8}$? $\frac{3}{8}$ = 3:8

5 Write $\frac{7}{10} + \frac{4}{5}$ as a mixed number. $1\frac{1}{2}$

6 $11 \div 0.11 =$ 100

7 $(1.5)^2 + 1.5 =$ 3.75

8 1.3099 becomes 1.310 when rounded to how many significant figures? 4

9 $6 < \sqrt{40} < 7$ TRUE or FALSE? TRUE

10 If $a = 2$, $b = 4$, $c = 3$ find the value of $5ab - c^3$ 13

11 $\frac{x^2}{x} = 4$, so $x =$ 4

12 What is the lowest common multiple of 6 and 10? 30

B

ANSWER

1 If 240 pencils cost £15 how many pencils for £6? 96

2 I put down 40% deposit on furniture costing £850. How much is left to pay? £ 510

3 120 g is approximately 4 oz

4 6 ft 6 in is approximately 2 m

5 A coach departs 22.35 and arrives 06.15. How long does the journey take? 7 h 40 min

6 The density of gold is 19 g/cm^3. A ring has a volume of 0.3 cm^3. What is its mass? 5.7 g

7 A bicycle wheel is 50 cm diameter. How far does it travel in 100 rotations? 157 m

8 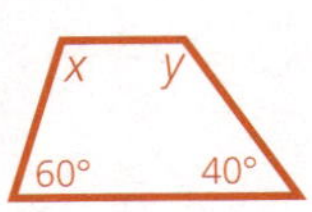

For the trapezium shown write down the size of angles x, y. $x =$ 120°, $y =$ 140°

9 
What is the number of axes of symmetry of this shape? 0

10 Express 2 h 25 min to the nearest half hour. $2\frac{1}{2}$ h

C

ANSWER

A driver takes his lorry over to France and back. There are two ferries he can use from Portsmouth and two to return from St. Malo. The table shows the ferry departure times and crossing times.

Cross-channel Ferry Portsmouth – St. Malo	
Departure times from Portsmouth to St. Malo	7.30 am 9.00 pm
Crossing time	8 h 55 min
Departure times from St. Malo to Portsmouth	10.45 am 9.25 pm
Crossing time	8 h 41 min

The driver departs on the early morning ferry from Portsmouth. It takes him 43 min to disembark the ferry at St. Malo and 85 min to drive to the city of Rennes, 70 km away. He then spends 1 h 45 min in Rennes unloading and a further 1 h 22 min driving back to St. Malo.

1 How long is the sea crossing to St. Malo? 8 h 55 min

2 At what time does the morning ferry from Portsmouth arrive in St. Malo? 4.25 pm

3 How long does it take to disembark the ferry and drive to Rennes? 2 h 8 min

4 At what time does the lorry arrive in Rennes? 6.33 pm

5 How long does it take to travel from Portsmouth to Rennes? 11 h 3 min

6 How long does it take to unload and drive back to St. Malo? 3 h 7 min

7 At what time does the driver get back to St. Malo from Rennes? 9.40 pm

8 Is he in time to catch the evening ferry back to Portsmouth? No

9 What is the departure time of the next ferry he can take to return to Portsmouth? 10.45 am

10 How long is the return sea crossing to Portsmouth? 8 h 41 min

11 At what time does the driver arrive back at Portsmouth? 7.26 pm

12 How long has the whole journey taken, from Portsmouth back to Portsmouth? 35 h 56 min

Section 3 Test 10

A

		ANSWER
1	$-5 \times 5 =$	-25
2	$\frac{24 \times 45}{9 \times 8} =$	15
3	Write $2^{(5-2)}$ as (a) a power of two	(a) 2^3
	(b) a number.	(b) 8
4	Express 35:63 as a fraction in its lowest terms.	$\frac{5}{9}$
5	$3\frac{3}{4} - 1\frac{7}{8} =$	$1\frac{7}{8}$
6	$0.1 \times 0.02 \times 0.003 =$	0.000006
7	$(1^2 + 0.1^2) - 1.01 =$	0
8	Round 0.001757 to (a) 2 decimal places	(a) 0.00
	(b) 2 significant figures.	(b) 0.0018
9	$9 < \sqrt{90} < 10$ TRUE or FALSE?	TRUE
10	If $x = 2$, $y = 3$ find the value of $(x + y)^2 - (x^2 + y^2)$	12
11	$\frac{9}{m} = m$, $m =$	3
12	$2^4 + 1$ is a prime number. TRUE or FALSE?	TRUE

B

		ANSWER
1	Find the cost of 360 envelopes if 45 cost £1.	£ 8
2	I buy 12 sweaters for £95 and sell them at £12·50 each. What is my profit?	£ 55
3	900 g is approximately	2 lb
4	2.5 m is approximately	8 ft
5	Anwar leaves at 09.50 on a journey lasting $6\frac{1}{2}$ hours. When does he arrive?	16.20
6	A cork of mass 2.88 g has a volume of 12 cm^3. What is the density of cork?	0.24 g/cm^3
7	5 m^3 of concrete is used to lay a path 2 m wide and 10 cm thick. How long is the path?	25 m
8	 The line *AT* is a tangent to the circle centre *O*. What size is angle *OTA*? $\angle OTA =$	90°
9	 What is the order of rotational symmetry of this shape about its centre?	2
10	Express 588 seconds to the nearest minute.	10 min

C

ANSWER

Luke and Iram share a set of six number cards. Each card has a single digit on it.

Luke's three cards are:	**4**	**1**	**8**
and Iram's cards are:	**5**	**2**	**3**

Help Luke and Iram to arrange their cards to answer the following questions.

		ANSWER
1	What is the smallest three-digit number Luke can make?	1 4 8
2	What is the largest three-digit number Iram can make?	5 3 2
3	What is the largest three-digit even number Luke can make?	8 1 4
4	What is the smallest three-digit even number Iram can make?	3 5 2
5	What is the largest number exactly divisible by 5 that Iram can make?	3 2 5
6	Which two cards can Luke use to show a square number?	8 1
7	Which two cards can Iram use to show a power of two?	3 2
8	What is the largest prime number Iram can make with two of her cards?	5 3
9	What is the difference between Luke's largest three-digit number and Iram's smallest two-digit number?	818
10	What is the sum of Luke's smallest three-digit odd number and Iram's largest three-digit even number?	1013
11	Luke makes the smallest two-digit odd number he can. He then multiplies this number by the digit remaining on his third card. What answer does he get?	328
12	Iram makes the largest two-digit even number she can. She then divides this number by the digit remaining on her third card. What remainder does she get?	rem 1

Section 3 Test 11

A

		ANSWER
1	$-5 \times -5 =$	$+25$
2	$\frac{48 \times 66}{36} =$	88
3	Write $3^5 \times 3^3$ as a power of three.	3^8
4	Insert the symbol <, > or = to make a correct statement.	$58\% < \frac{5}{8}$
5	$\frac{2}{3} + 2\frac{1}{2} =$	$3\frac{1}{6}$
6	$0.3 \div 0.2 =$	1.5
7	$(1 + 0.1)^2 - 1.01 =$	0.2
8	0.002659 becomes 0.0027 when rounded to 4 significant figures. TRUE or FALSE?	FALSE
9	$25 < \sqrt{250} < 50$ TRUE or FALSE?	FALSE
10	If $a = 30$, $b = 40$, $c = 12$ find the value of $\frac{2a}{c} + \frac{3b}{a}$	9
11	$w^2 + 4^2 = 5^2$, so $w =$	3
12	$(2 \times 3)^2 - (2^3 + 3^3) =$	1

B

		ANSWER
1	I save £14·50 per month. How much have I saved in 1 year?	£ 174
2	I buy 495 American dollars for £330. How many dollars do I get for each £1?	1.5 dollars
3	1600 m is approximately	1 mile
4	1350 mm × 5 =	6.750 m
5	How many years between the start of 1 BC and the end of 1 AD?	2 years
6	The speed of a glacier is 0.05 mm/s. How far does it travel in 1 day?	4.32 m
7	A regular hexagon fits exactly inside a circle 20 cm in diameter. How long is the perimeter of the hexagon?	60 cm
8	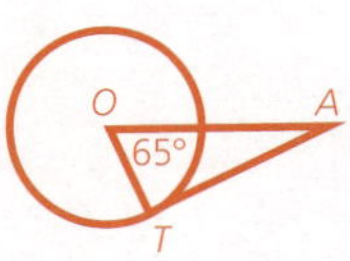 O is the centre of the circle and AT is a tangent. What size is angle *OAT*? ∠*OAT* =	25°
9	 The word OXO is written diagonally across a square. How many axes of symmetry are there for the word and square as a whole?	2
10	If 55 identical bottles can be filled from a 250 litre container, what is the approximate capacity of a bottle to the nearest half litre?	$4\frac{1}{2}$ ℓ

C

Mrs Fisher takes her two children Lee and Carrie out for a meal. The restaurant is serving a three course meal. The menu from which they can choose is shown below.

> ***Eat Well Restaurant***
>
> Starter Course
> *Soup*
> *Melon*
>
> Main Course
> *Beef*
> *Chicken*
> *Salmon*
>
> Sweet Course
> *Gateau*
> *Trifle*
> *Ice-cream*

Lee orders his meal first.

		ANSWER
1	In how many ways can Lee choose his starter course?	2
2	In how many ways can Lee choose his main course?	3
3	How many different combinations of starter course and main course can Lee choose from?	2 × 3 = 6
4	In how many ways can Lee choose his sweet course?	3
5	How many different combinations of all three courses can Lee choose from?	2 × 3 × 3 = 18

Lee chose soup for his starter, chicken for his main course and ice-cream for the sweet. When Carrie orders her meal she decides to make a different choice on every course from that of her brother.

		ANSWER
6	Write down a possible choice for Carrie's meal. Starter	Melon
	Main	Salmon or Beef
	Sweet	Gateau or Trifle
7	In how many ways could Carrie choose her starter course?	1
8	In how many ways could Carrie choose her main course?	2
9	In how many ways could Carrie choose her sweet course?	2
10	How many different combinations of all three courses could Carrie choose from?	1 × 2 × 2 = 4

When Mrs Fisher makes her choice she decides to differ from both her children but then discovers she cannot do this on every course.

		ANSWER
11	On which course MUST she choose the same as EITHER Lee OR Carrie?	Starter
12	In how many ways could Mrs Fisher choose each of her other two courses?	1

Section 3 Test 12

A — ANSWER

1 $(-5)^2 = \underline{-5} \times \underline{-5} =$ 25

2 $\frac{54 \times 56}{63} =$ 48

3 Write $3^5 \div 3^3$ as a power of three. 3^2

4 Insert <, > or = to make a correct statement. $1\frac{1}{8}$ < 1.8 = $1\frac{4}{5}$

5 $3\frac{1}{3} \times 10 =$ $33\frac{1}{3}$

6 $0.48 \div 0.06 =$ 8

7 $(0.2)^2 + (0.3)^2 + (0.2 + 0.3)^2 =$ 0.38

8 0.0387 becomes 0.0390 when rounded to three decimal places. TRUE or FALSE? FALSE

9 $6 < \frac{278}{39} < 8$ TRUE or FALSE? TRUE

10 If $x = 3$, $y = 5$, $z = 8$ find the value of $\frac{z}{1 + xy}$. 0.5

11 $50 = \frac{1}{2}a \times 5^2$, so a = 4

12 Write in the next two terms of the sequence. $\frac{1}{2}$, $\frac{2}{3}$, $\frac{3}{4}$, $\frac{4}{5}$, $\frac{5}{6}$, $\frac{6}{7}$

B — ANSWER

1 Which is the better buy (a) 40 for 50p or (b) 200 for £2·40? (b)

2 A £395 carpet is reduced by 8%. What is the amount saved? £ 31·60

3 5 miles is approximately 8 km

4 13.53 kg ÷ 6 = 2255 g

5 Frank works 5 shifts each of 7 h 50 min. What is Frank's total working time? 39 h 10 min

6 What mass of Helium of density 0.18 kg/m^3 is needed to fill a 250 m^3 balloon? 45 kg

7 A square is drawn to fit exactly inside a circle of 40 cm diameter. Find the area of the square. 800 cm^2

8 

O is the centre of the circle. What size is angle x? x = 40°

9 
What is (a) the number of axes of symmetry and (b) the order of rotational symmetry about the centre of the shape shown? (a) 1 (b) 1

10 If 720 equal lengths of electrical cable are cut from a reel of total length 500 yards, what is the length of each cut piece of cable to the nearest foot? 2 ft

C — ANSWER

Javad has fourteen cards.

On six of them is a single digit number.

3	6	5	1	0	2

On each of the other eight is a mathematical symbol.

+	−	×	÷	=	·	<	>

Fill in the blanks to show how Javad arranged his cards to answer the following questions. Not every card needs to be used but no card can be used twice in any one question.

1 3 × 2 = 6

2 5 + 3 − 2 = 6

3 3 0 ÷ 6 = 5

4 6 0 ÷ 5 = 1 2

5 3 0 − 6 < 2 5

6 3 6 ÷ 1 2 > 0

7 3 ÷ 2 = 1 · 5

8 5 = 6 ÷ 1 · 2

9 2 × 3 ÷ 1 + 0 = 6

10 2 6 = 3 0 − 5 + 1

11 1 ÷ 0 · 5 = 2

12 3 ÷ 0 · 2 = 1 5

Section 3 Revision Test

		ANSWER
1	Write down the remainder when the square of 8 is divided by 12.	rem 4
2	$\frac{2}{3}(65 - 56) =$	6
3	What is the value of $2^7 \div 2^4$?	8
4	Express 24% as a ratio in its lowest terms.	6 : 25
5	Write 24% of 35 as a decimal.	8.4
6	$2 \times 0.2 \times 0.02 =$	0.008
7	$\frac{1}{0.2}(1 - 0.2) =$	4
8	0.00398 becomes 0.004 when rounded to three significant figures. TRUE or FALSE ?	FALSE
9	$\frac{0.1}{0.2} < \frac{0.3}{0.4} < \frac{0.5}{0.6}$ TRUE or FALSE ?	TRUE
10	If $a = 2$, $b = 3$, $c = 0$, find the value of $a^3 - \frac{bc}{a}$.	8
11	$\frac{27}{x^2} = x$, so $x =$	3
12	Write in the next three terms of the sequence. 2, 3, 5, 7, 11, 13, 17, 19,	23 , 29 , 31
13	If I buy 40 litres of petrol at 64.5p per litre, how much change will I get from £30?	£ 4·20
14	The price of a car costing £12 450 rises by 4%. What is the new price of the car?	£ 12 948
15	Which is the larger quantity, (a) 2 litres or (b) half a gallon?	(b)
16	Which is the longer length, (a) 2 metres or (b) 6 feet?	(a)
17	A late-night TV programme begins at 11.35 p.m. and ends at a quarter to two in the morning. How long is the programme?	130 min
18	Kieran runs 100 m in 12 seconds. What is his speed in km/h?	30 km/h
19	A delivery van has a load space measuring 1.8 m wide, 2 m high and 2.4 m long. How many parcels each measuring 50 cm × 60 cm × 80 cm can be fitted inside?	36
20	A parallelogram is drawn so that its smallest angle is one third the size of its largest angle. How big is the largest angle?	135°
21	Which letters of the word TORCH have one and only one axis of symmetry?	T, C
22	Find the area of a lawn measuring 11.85 m long and 6.05 m wide to the nearest square metre.	72 m^2
23	A point *P* has coordinates (–2, 5). It is translated by the mapping $(x, y) \longrightarrow (x + 3, y + 3)$. What are the new coordinates of point *P*?	(1 , 8)
24	On a map of scale 1:50 000, two towns are 12 cm apart. What is the actual distance between the two towns in km?	6 km
25	12 coloured balls are placed in a bag. 3 are red, 4 are blue and the remainder are green. If one ball is taken from the bag, what is the probability that it will be green?	$\frac{5}{12}$

Section 3 Revision Test

ANSWER

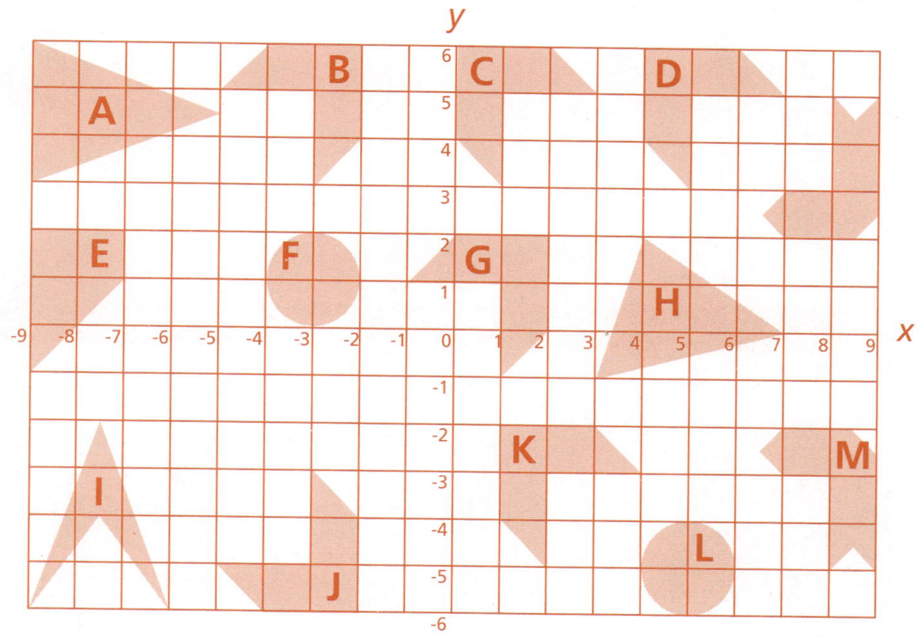

26	Write down the coordinates of each corner of triangle H.	(3 , –1) (4 , 2) (7 , 0)
27	Write down the coordinates of one corner of shape G that have a negative *x*-value.	(–1 , 1)
28	Write down the coordinates of one corner of shape G that have a negative *y*-value.	(1 , –1)
29	Write down the coordinates of the mid-point of the shortest side of triangle A.	(–9 , 4.5)
30	Write down the coordinates of one corner of shape I that have equal size *x*-value and *y*-value.	(–6 , –6)
31	Which circle, F or L, has centre coordinates such that the sum of the *x*-value and the *y*-value is zero?	L
32	Which of the following, if any, is a reflection of shape B in the *y*-axis? Choose from: C, D, G, K, J or NONE.	NONE
33	Which of the following, if any, is a reflection of shape B in the *x*-axis? Choose from: C, D, G, K, J or NONE.	J
34	On the grid above, sketch in the reflection of shape M in the *x*-axis.	
35	Which of the following, if any, is a translation of shape B? Choose from: C, D, G, K, J or NONE.	G
36	Write down the mapping that will translate shape K to position D. $(x,y) \longrightarrow$	$(x + 3 , y + 8)$
37	Write down the mapping that will translate the centre of circle F to the origin. $(x,y) \longrightarrow$	$(x + 3 , y - 1)$
38	Which shape has the larger area, K or M?	K
39	Which shape has exactly half the area of shape A?	I
40	Which of the following shapes have the same area as shape E? Choose from: B, D, F, H or M.	B and D

Mental Arithmetic

Develops mental maths skills through carefully graded, weekly tests

Titles available: Introductory Book, Books 1–6; Teacher's Introductory Book, Teacher's Books 1–6

Other series from Schofield & Sims Ltd:

	Maths & Science	Language & Literacy
Early Learning	**Workbooks:** Nursery Activity Books	**Workbooks:** Early Writing Books, Nursery Activity Books, Nursery Writing Books
Key Stage 1	**Workbooks:** Key Maths Number Books	**Workbooks:** Basic Skills, Sound Practice **Readers:** Play Words, Read with the Riddlers, Read and Colour **Dictionaries:** Picture Dictionary, My First Picture Dictionary **Word books:** Picture Words, Early Words, Topic Words **Copymasters:** Reading Comprehension KS 1
Bridging Key Stages 1 & 2	**Workbooks:** Starting Science **Programmes:** Maths Quest **Games:** Master Pieces	**Workbooks:** Early Spellings **Programmes:** Journeys in Reading, Oracy, Study Reading **Dictionaries:** Illustrated Dictionary, Bilingual Dictionaries **Word books:** First Words, Early Words **Copymasters:** Reading Comprehension Bridging Pack **Games:** Master Pieces
Key Stage 2	**Workbooks:** **Mental Arithmetic,** Homework, Progress Papers – Maths **Practice:** Number Practice, Alpha/Beta, More Practice **Assessment:** Assessment Papers in Maths, Assessment Papers in Science, Practice SATs – Maths	**Workbooks:** Springboard, Spellaway, Key Spellings, Homework, Spelling Practice, Progress Papers – English, Progress Papers – Reasoning **Programmes:** English Skills **Dictionaries:** Keyword Dictionary, Easy Dictionary, Concise Junior Dictionary, Basic Dictionary, Compact Dictionary, Simplified Dictionary, Spelling Dictionary **Word books:** Better Words, In Other Words, Choose Your Words, Use Your Words, Classified Spelling **Assessments:** Assessment Papers in English, Practice SATs – Explorers, Practice SATs – Bicycles **Copymasters:** Reading Comprehension KS 2, English Practice

Schofield & Sims Ltd, Huddersfield, England
Tel: 01484 607080 Fax: 01484 606815

ISBN 0-7217-2449-3
9 780721 724492